THE GREAT LIVES SERIES

Here are the life stories of courageous men and women from all walks of life, in every corner of the globe, who have challenged the way society thinks, stood up for their rights, and changed the world. Whether fighting for racial, social, or economic justice and freedom, these history makers have won victories that were once thought to be impossible, and have inspired hope when all were hopeless. They can still teach all of us unforgettable lessons by the very fact of their great lives.

Other biographies in the Great Lives Series

CLARA BARTON: *Founder of the American Red Cross*
CESAR CHAVEZ: *Hope for the People*
CHRISTOPHER COLUMBUS: *The Intrepid Mariner*
AMELIA EARHART: *Challenging the Skies*
THOMAS EDISON: *Inventing the Future*
JOHN GLENN: *Space Pioneer*
MIKHAIL GORBACHEV: *The Soviet Innovator*
JESSE JACKSON: *A Voice for Change*
THOMAS JEFFERSON: *The Philosopher President*
JOHN F. KENNEDY: *Courage in Crisis*
MARTIN LUTHER KING: *Dreams for a Nation*
ABRAHAM LINCOLN: *The Freedom President*
GOLDA MEIR: *A Leader in Peace and War*
NELSON MANDELA: *A Voice Set Free*
SANDRA DAY O'CONNOR: *A New Justice, a New Voice*
SALLY RIDE: *Shooting for the Stars*
FRANKLIN D. ROOSEVELT: *The People's President*
HARRIET TUBMAN: *Call to Freedom*
THE WRIGHT BROTHERS: *Conquering the Sky*
LECH WALESA: *The Road to Democracy*
LEWIS AND CLARK: *Leading America West*

GREAT LIVES

THURGOOD MARSHALL

Champion of Civil Rights

Elisabeth Krug

FAWCETT COLUMBINE
NEW YORK

For middle-school readers

A Fawcett Columbine Book
Published by Ballantine Books

Library of Congress Catalog Card Number: 92-90396

ISBN 0-449-90731-7

Cover design by Georgia Morrissey
Cover illustration by Ann Meisel

Manufactured in the United States of America

First Edition: February 1993

10 9 8 7 6 5 4 3 2 1

TABLE OF CONTENTS

Chapter 1
Mr. Civil Rights   1

Chapter 2
Baltimore   6

Chapter 3
College Years   19

Chapter 4
A Legal Whiz   30

Chapter 5
"The Time Is Ripe"   45

Chapter 6
Jim Crow Must Go   59

Chapter 7
Brown v. Board of Education   77

Chapter 8
The Aftermath of *Brown*   94

Chapter 9
Solicitor General of the United States   111

Chapter 10
Justice Thurgood Marshall   122

Chapter 11
   A Legacy of Hope   133

Bibliography   147

THURGOOD MARSHALL

COLLECTION OF THE SUPREME COURT OF THE UNITED STATES

1

Mr. Civil Rights

AN AIR OF expectation swept the packed chamber of the U.S. Supreme Court on December 8, 1953. Today the justices would listen to two great attorneys battle to win the most celebrated lawsuit in the nation, *Brown v. Board of Education of Topeka, Kansas*. The victor would affect the future of millions of African-American schoolchildren barred from attending schools with whites. At no time in recent history had race relations reached such a critical juncture in the courts.

Heads looked up to see a tall, dark-skinned attorney enter the room and take a seat at the lawyers' table. To the hundreds of African-Americans seated in the courtroom and lined up in the halls and walkways outside, the forty-five-year-old man was a hero. His name was Thurgood Marshall, and he was about to argue one of the most important cases in U.S. history.

Brown v. Board of Education (*v.* means "versus" or "against") capped years of effort by Marshall to smash open the legal barricades of single-race schools. In arguing *Brown*, he wanted to prove that Topeka's board of education denied its black children their constitu-

1

tional rights by forcing them into all-black schools. On one side of the argument were African-American parents and children tired of being told that blacks were forbidden to mix with whites in school. Opposing them were white school officials who said that segregation, or separation of the races, was lawful and here to stay.

Ever since 1896, when the Supreme Court ruled in *Plessy v. Ferguson* that it was lawful to divide blacks and whites into "separate but equal" facilities, Southern officials had separated the races in their schools. But the "separate" schools were rarely "equal." Schools for white children got greater funding, more teachers, and much better facilities than did black schools, which were often dilapidated structures without heat, electricity, or plumbing.

In 1950 Rev. Oliver Brown had seen enough of "separate but equal" in his hometown in Kansas. Each morning his seven-year-old daughter, Linda, had to cross dangerous train tracks to go the long distance to her school. There was another public school close to her home, but Linda could not go to it because she was black. Thinking this unfair, Mr. Brown contacted a civil rights organization known as the National Association for the Advancement of Colored People (NAACP). He was soon under the expert guidance of its top lawyer, Thurgood Marshall. Eventually Brown's case made its way to the Supreme Court.

The Reverend Mr. Brown and the other black parents could not have chosen a lawyer better qualified than Thurgood Marshall. A graduate of Howard University Law School, Marshall had spent the last twenty-two years fighting for the rights of African-Americans. In a recent spate of Supreme Court victories, the attorney had got black students admitted to previously restricted white graduate schools. Now he wanted to tackle the nation's grade and high schools.

At six feet two inches and over two hundred pounds, the large-framed, mustachioed attorney presented an imposing figure. Freedom Built on Law was his motto, and he had won an impressive amount of freedom for his clients. Because of his outstanding record, thousands of admirers called him Mr. Civil Rights. Marshall had experienced segregation's yoke firsthand. As a boy he attended a substandard, overcrowded grade school. He was told to stay away from whites-only parks, theaters, and washrooms. Later he was refused admission to the graduate school of his choice because of the color of his skin. Determined to change this unfair treatment of African-Americans, Marshall, the great-grandson of a slave, armed himself with the principles of the U.S. legal system. He held up the Constitution as his Bible and defended it with the zeal of a crusader.

The Constitution guaranteed equal rights to African-Americans in the Fourteenth Amendment, passed after the Civil War. Yet, during the nearly two hundred years that followed, judges and politicians had watered down its mandate. They interpreted its provision for "equal protection of the laws" to mean "*separate* but *equal* protection of the laws." Knowing that this was done to keep blacks in their place, Marshall set out to prove that "separate but equal" was unconstitutional.

He was aware that he would have a difficult time winning the justices over to his side. The Court had upheld the *Plessy* doctrine for nearly half a century. Moreover, the justices were impressed by Marshall's influential opponent, John W. Davis. A former presidential candidate, congressman, and ambassador, the white-haired gentleman from the South had argued more cases before the Supreme Court than any lawyer in the twentieth century. Davis was out to prove that segregation was a time-honored practice of states that was beyond the jurisdiction of the federal government.

When Marshall's turn came to speak, he launched into firm but impassioned prose. He described the terrible toll segregation took on black children. The racist practice, he told the Court, imposed a "badge of inferiority" on those children that forever hindered their chances for success. After Marshall sat down, Davis took the podium to give one of the most inspired performances of his career. Davis's grasp of constitutional history impressed everyone, including Marshall.

After the three arduous days of hearings, Marshall waited anxiously for the justices' vote on the case. It did not come. In the weeks and months that followed, it still did not come. Finally, five months later, on May 17, 1954, the Supreme Court handed down its decision. Speaking for all the justices, Chief Justice Earl Warren said, "Does segregation of children in public schools solely on the basis of race . . . deprive the children . . . of equal educational opportunities?" Marshall held his breath as the chief justice delivered the startling answer to the question. "We believe that it does. We conclude that in the field of education 'separate but equal' has no place." In fifteen dramatic minutes the Court had outlawed segregation and reconfigured the social fabric of the nation. Marshall rushed from the courtroom to spread the news. It was the greatest moment of his life.

In the initial round of excitement, Marshall had no time to think of the problems that lay ahead. The decision incited the anger of Southern segregationists, who labeled the day Black Monday. Fiery crosses of hatred lit by the Ku Klux Klan prefigured the violent reaction that was to come. Thurgood Marshall's struggle to overcome such hatred and violence, and to wage the valiant struggle for civil rights, earned him a place as one of the great men in history.

2

Baltimore

THURGOOD MARSHALL WAS born in Baltimore, Maryland, on July 2, 1908. That summer a white mob in Springfield, Illinois, rioted against blacks, killing two of them. These murders took place less than two miles from Abraham Lincoln's grave. The great president had freed the slaves, but he couldn't protect blacks from the wave of violence they endured after the Civil War. Alarmed by the high rate of lynchings, or murders, of African-Americans, a group of blacks and whites met in New York City to do something about it. Out of their conferences, held May 30 and June 1, 1909, the National Association for the Advancement of Colored People (NAACP) was formed. The NAACP went on to win major battles in the fight against violence and discrimination against African-Americans. Leading the NAACP through its greatest victories on the legal front was Thurgood Marshall.

The baby born to the Marshalls in 1908 wasn't the first in his family to become an activist for the rights of African-Americans. Thurgood came from a long line of proud and defiant people. His parents, Norma Arica and William Canfield Marshall, were well educated and held high ambitions for Thurgood and his older brother, Aubrey. Thurgood's mother was a kindergarten teacher who made sure the boys got home on time for supper and did their homework. She had received her diploma from an all-black Maryland college and earned teaching credits at Columbia University's Teachers College in New York City. Thurgood's father was an amateur writer who worked as a dining-car waiter on the Baltimore & Ohio Railroad. Later he landed a better job as chief steward at the elegant all-white Gibson Island Club on Chesapeake Bay.

A self-taught man, William Marshall didn't have much formal education. He was fortunate to have jobs with decent pay and he worked hard. On his days off he spent hours pursuing his real interest, courtroom law. As a spectator at trials he soaked up the legal procedure and arguments that sent people to jail or gave them their freedom. William Marshall sometimes took Thurgood and Aubrey to court with him. At night, seated around the dinner table, the three would debate legal issues and current events. By constantly challenging his sons on points they made, William Marshall sharpened their skills and arguments. "He never told me to become a lawyer," Marshall recalled later, "but he turned me into one. He did it by teaching me to argue, by challenging my logic on every point, by making me prove every statement I made."

If William Marshall had been given an opportunity to study law, he probably would have been the family's first great lawyer. As it was, he scored a notable victory in becoming the first African-American to serve on a Baltimore grand jury. After only three days in his new post he convinced his fellow jurors to stop asking whether the accused were white or black. He thought the question was unfair, especially since blacks were more likely than whites to be convicted of crimes.

Like William Marshall, the rest of Thurgood's family was proud of its African-American heritage and was prepared to speak up for it. As a boy Thurgood loved to hear stories about the headstrong members of his family. His favorite tale centered around his mother's grandfather. According to Marshall, his great-grandfather had been abducted from a part of Africa known as the Congo (now the Republic of Zaire). He was brought to the eastern shore of Maryland to work on a plantation. However, he grew to be so cantankerous that his owner decided he couldn't keep him. He couldn't sell him, either, out of pity for anyone who would have to put up with him. The plantation owner had no choice but to let the mean slave go free. He did just that, on condition that the unruly African never show his face in that part of Maryland again. "That," Marshall said proudly, "was the only time Massuh didn't get an argument from the old boy." Marshall's great-grandfather didn't pay much attention to the parting words of his master. Instead he boldly settled down a few miles from the white man's plantation. He lived there until the day he died, and according to Marshall, "nobody ever laid a hand on him."

Marshall's delight in telling this story downplayed his familiarity with the cruel practice of slavery. Half of the Africans captured and sent to America on ships died en route. Upon arrival they were sold at auctions, like cattle. Except for the lucky few whose owners were lenient, they were forced to work from sunup to sundown. They were frequently beaten, raped, or killed. Aware of the terrible fate of most slaves, Marshall took pride in the fact that his great-grandfather stood up to his master, who had the power and authority to kill him.

Thurgood was named after the grandfather on his father's side of the family. Grandfather Marshall was a free man. When the Civil War broke out between the North and the South in 1861, he signed up with the Northern forces to fight against slavery. Known simply as Marshall before the war, he learned that he needed to add a first name in order to enlist. He chose Thoroughgood. In this way Thoroughgood Marshall became one of the 186,000 brave African-Americans to serve in the Union army and risk their lives for their country. An African-American who fought in the Civil War faced ordeals far worse than those endured by his white compatriots. In going into battle in the South, he ventured into the territory of servitude, where hatred of freed blacks ran high. If caught by the Confederate army, the black soldier faced torture and death or a return to slavery. Approximately 38,000 African-American soldiers died in the Civil War.

Fortunately Thoroughgood Marshall was not one of those who died. After the war he married a woman named Annie, whose skin was so light that Marshall never knew whether she was black or white. Annie Marshall's feisty spirit matched her husband's. The two of them opened a grocery store in Baltimore. When the local electric company decided to install a light pole on the strip of land in front of their store, Mrs. Marshall parked herself in a chair over the targeted spot. She remained there until the electric company gave up and placed the pole in a neighbor's yard.

9

Telling this anecdote later, Marshall boasted, "Grandma Annie emerged as the victor of what may have been the first successful sit-down strike in Maryland."

Marshall was equally impressed by his bold grandparents on his mother's side. Like the Marshalls, they owned a large grocery store in Baltimore, which Thurgood often visited as a child. In his early days Grandfather Isaiah Williams had worked as a sailor and traveled to different parts of the world. An avowed opera lover, he never forgot a visit he made once to the Chilean port of Arica. There he was treated to a fine performance of Vincenzo Bellini's opera *Norma*. It was so fine that the sailor later named his daughter after both the opera and the town. For the rest of her life, Thurgood's mother held on to the name Norma Arica. In addition to an operatic name, Norma Marshall inherited her father's love of music. She was admired for her ability to sing and play the piano, and she sometimes appeared in local opera and theater productions.

In the 1870s, just after the Civil War, Isaiah Williams organized a public rally to protest police brutality toward African-Americans. The demonstration proved to authorities that the black community was willing to speak out against abuse. Challenging white officials was no easy matter in the days following the Civil War. Extremist groups including the notorious Ku Klux Klan terrorized and murdered "uppity" African-Americans. On all government levels officials ignored these acts of violence. They turned their backs on the rights and needs of African-Americans. Congress passed problack civil rights legislation between 1866 and 1875. But after the Supreme Court ruled the laws unconstitutional, lawmakers around the country felt free to enact segregation ordinances that separated whites and blacks.

These ordinances were known as Jim Crow laws, so named after a song sung by Thomas Rice in a popular nineteenth-century minstrel show. During the performance Jim Crow, played by a white actor who blackened his face, sang these words: "Wheel about, turn about, do just so. Every time I wheel about, I jump Jim Crow." The term *Jim Crow* came to stand for the denigration of African-Americans.

Jim Crow segregation laws did just that. They set up separate, and usually inferior, trains, hotels, drinking fountains, schools, restaurants, and neighborhoods for African-Americans. Separated from their darker brethren, whites deepened their mistrust and criticism of them. White lawmakers went to great lengths to keep blacks "in their place" and at a distance. Officials in Birmingham, Alabama, went so far as to outlaw games of checkers and dominoes between black and white players. In several school districts in the South, schoolchildren of one race were forbidden to use textbooks previously read by the other. Once segregation took hold after the Civil War, it spread, like a hungry vine, into the social and political foundations of America. By the time Thurgood Marshall was born, segregation was a way of life.

In many ways Thurgood was lucky to grow up in Baltimore. It was rich in history and teeming with big-city life. At Fort McHenry, where Baltimore defeated the British in battle during the War of 1812, Francis Scott Key got the inspiration for "The Star-Spangled Banner." The city achieved equal notoriety for being the birthplace of baseball legend Babe Ruth. After joining Baltimore's professional team, Ruth played his first game as a member of the International League in 1914, the year Marshall entered first grade.

Another Baltimore native who made history when Thurgood was young was the great satirist H. L. Mencken. In his newspaper articles for the *Baltimore Sun*, Mencken attacked everything from corruption to antiblack city ordinances. Though white, he supported many problack causes. As editor of the literary magazine *The American Mercury*, he first published many of the talented black writers of the day.

Jazz bands also flourished in Baltimore during Thurgood's youth. At the Marsh Market dance halls down by the harbor, black musicians played their way to fame. Standing out among them was piano player Eubie Blake, the celebrated ragtime improviser and show-tune composer. Another well-loved musician was Chuck Webb, who led the "hottest" swing band in the country. Webb's band was so good that it was the only jazz band invited to perform at the Metropolitan Opera House in New York.

Yet, overshadowing the exciting atmosphere of Baltimore was the sad fact of racism. Babe Ruth played astounding baseball, but he played for an all-white team. African-Americans weren't allowed into the major leagues until 1947, when Jackie Robinson played his first game for the Brooklyn Dodgers. Racism affected African-Americans in other ways as well. Chuck Webb dazzled the world with his music, but he died of tuberculosis, the number-one killer of African-Americans. The disease spread fast in the city's black ghettoes, where poverty-stricken people had little food and heat. In Baltimore the death rate among blacks was twice that of whites.

Sandwiched between the North and the South, Baltimore was a mix of both parts of the country. Before the Civil War the city prospered as a slave market, yet it also gave birth to a strong abolitionist (antislavery) movement that kept strong ties to the North. After the war Baltimore adopted a Northern economy based largely on shipping and manufacturing, but its social organization remained strictly Southern. As in the South, relations between blacks and whites were governed by the sinister hand of Jim Crow. "The only thing different between the South and Baltimore was trolley cars," Marshall recalled. "They weren't segregated. Everything else was segregated."

For young Thurgood segregation meant that he had to go to an inferior, all-black grade school and stay out of the "whites only" sections of public parks and beaches. He could never see the latest hit movies because African-Americans weren't allowed into the white theaters where they were shown. Black theaters obtained only cheap prints of second runs. The few theaters that admitted blacks sat them so far back that they could hardly see the stage. Thurgood wasn't even allowed to use a public rest room downtown—they were all reserved for whites. He discovered this humiliating fact during a moment of need one day on a trip downtown. After searching the entire area for a rest room that didn't have a WHITES ONLY sign, he went home. He never forgot the experience.

Baltimore was one of the first cities in the United States to adopt laws that forbid blacks to own or rent homes on blocks where whites lived. Several black families bold enough to defy these laws were greeted with rocks thrown at them by their white neighbors. In 1920 the Supreme Court found the city ordinances unconstitutional. Yet blacks continued to be shut out of white neighborhoods by the silent agreement of realtors, homeowners, developers, and banks. Home-buyers often signed contracts pledging that they would not sell or rent to blacks. These unfair agreements, known as restrictive covenants, were common throughout the South.

Years later Thurgood Marshall led the successful fight against restrictive covenants and other discriminatory practices. During his youth, however, he had to live by the unfair rules and hope he could stay out of trouble. His parents helped by sheltering him as much as possible from the damaging effects of racism. In this effort they were relatively fortunate. Most of Baltimore's African-American families could not afford decent housing and had to live in poverty-ridden areas known as ghettoes. Will and Norma Marshall, though, pulled in enough money from their jobs to afford to live on a respectable street called Druid Hill Avenue, lined with pleasant, three-story brick houses.

Thurgood's childhood in the house on Druid Hill Avenue was warm and stable. Family friends described him as a happy child who had a serious, thoughtful side to him. "I can still see him coming down Division Street every Sunday afternoon at about one o'clock," recalled a family acquaintance. "He'd be wearing knee pants with both hands dug way into his pockets and be kicking a stone in front of him as he crossed over to Dolphin Street to visit his grandparents at their big grocery store on the corner. He was deep in study, that boy, and it was plain something was going on inside him." Though he was timid as a toddler, Marshall grew to be a "pretty tough guy" by the time he was five, according to his aunt. By the age of seven he had his first job, running errands for Hale's Market.

It was at about this time that Thurgood had his first conscious run-in with racism. On the playground one day he heard someone call a Jewish boy "kike." When Thurgood asked the boy why he didn't fight back at the person who insulted him, the boy asked Thurgood how he would respond if someone called him a "nigger." Would he fight? Thurgood had never heard the word *nigger* before. "I knew *kike* was a dirty word," he recalled later, "but I hadn't known about *nigger*. I went home and wanted to know right that minute what this all meant." Thurgood's father not only explained the racist term, he gave Thurgood instructions on how to respond to it in the future. "Anyone calls you nigger," he told his son, "you not only got my permission to fight him—you got my orders to fight him."

By this time Thurgood was in elementary school, experiencing racism's effect firsthand. Like nearly every education system in the country, Baltimore schools typified the failure of the "separate but equal" doctrine upheld by the Supreme Court in its famous *Plessy* decision in 1896. Black and white schools in the city were separate, but hardly equal. Between 1898 and 1915, when Thurgood was seven years old, the city of Baltimore did not build any schools for African-American children. Instead it allotted them old, abandoned, or officially "unfit" buildings. Unlike their white counterparts, black schools were poorly equipped and overcrowded. Many held half-time classes to try to fit in all the students. Moreover, black teachers received less pay than did equally qualified whites and had no regular schedule of promotion.

Both Thurgood and his brother, Aubrey, attended the school in which their mother taught kindergarten. Even with his mother so near, though, Thurgood got into plenty of mischief. Boisterous and high-spirited, he found it difficult to concentrate on his school work and earned mediocre grades. Later, in high school, when he misbehaved in class, Thurgood was sent out of the classroom and told to memorize parts of the United States Constitution. By the time he graduated, he knew the whole document by heart.

Thurgood brought his wild streak home from school every afternoon, when he would spend time with the rowdy boys in the back alleys of his neighborhood. "We lived on a respectable street," he said later, "but behind us there were back alleys where the roughnecks and the tough kids hung out. When it was time for dinner, my mother used to go to the front door and call my older brother. Then she'd go to the *back* door and call me." Fortunately for Thurgood, Norma Marshall was strict enough to keep him in line. She used to say to him, "Boy, you may be tall, but if you get mean, I can always reach you with a chair."

During the time Thurgood was so tall that his mother couldn't reach him without a chair, he was in high school, growing to be over six feet in height. High school years were good ones for Marshall, largely because he attended a first-rate school. As luck would have it, Marshall's entry into high school coincided with Baltimore's citywide effort to upgrade its black schools. The showcase of this renewal project was Frederick Douglass High School, which Marshall entered as a freshman in the fall of 1921. Named after one of Maryland's former slaves who became a renowned spokesman for equal rights, Douglass High

16

came to symbolize new beginnings in race relations. As Baltimore's first black high school built to contemporary standards of the day, it boasted features many white students took for granted—electricity, central steam heat, multiple stairways, and bright, daylight-filled rooms. The school's reputation for excellence grew over the years, as many of its graduates went on to college and higher education. Though his grades didn't show it, Thurgood thrived at Douglass. He joined clubs, went to dances, and tried out for several sports teams.

After school and during vacations Thurgood worked at different jobs. One of them almost landed him behind bars because of an ugly incident that occurred when Thurgood was fourteen. The teenager was working as a delivery boy after school for Schoen's Specialty Shop. One day he carried a high stack of hat boxes to the trolley stop and waited for the train to arrive. When it did, Thurgood stepped forward into its opened doors. As he did so, he felt a sharp tug at his sleeve and heard a man hiss, "Nigguh, don't you never push in front of no white lady again." Within seconds Thurgood dropped the boxes, whirled around, and punched the man in the jaw. As the two succumbed to a fistfight, a white policeman came running toward them.

Thurgood would have been in serious trouble were it not for the fact that the policeman, Officer Matthews, was a racially tolerant man. After listening to both sides of the story, he eventually let Thurgood go. Considering that blacks were known to be beaten, jailed, or killed for striking a white man, Thurgood got off easy. He was even allowed to keep his job at Schoen's after news of the incident reached the shop.

Later, through his father's connections, he landed a high-paying job as a waiter on the B&O Railroad. On his first day of work for the railroad, the tall, slender teenager was given a pair of waiter's pants that were too short. When he asked for a longer pair, he was told by his boss, "Boy, we can get a man to fit the pants a lot easier than we can get pants to fit the man. Why don't you scroonch down a little more?" Realizing that he was just one of many available teenagers in need of a job, Marshall kept quiet. As he later put it, "I scroonched."

These humiliating incidents and others strengthened his resolve to fight for the respect he felt all African-Americans deserved. At first he used the only weapons he had—his fists. In years to come, though, his method would evolve into something far more powerful than a blow to the jaw. Marshall was about to discover the world of law. Using its tools of research, long-range planning, rhetoric, and logic, he went on to tackle not just one racist man, but a whole body of unjust legislation. As Marshall got older, he realized that words were stronger than weapons in his fight for justice.

3

College Years

AS MARSHALL'S CAREFREE high school days drew to a close, he was faced with the difficult task of choosing a college. Because white universities in the South refused to open their doors to blacks, and those in the North took in only a few of them, Marshall's choices were limited. Fortunately several black colleges had been founded as early as the mid-nineteenth century. One of the oldest and best among them was Lincoln University in Oxford, Pennsylvania, where Thurgood's brother, Aubrey, had just received his diploma. Since his parents thought highly of Lincoln, Marshall applied to the respected institution and was accepted. In the fall of 1925 he arrived, suitcase in hand, to join its freshman class.

Nestled in rural hills, Lincoln University was the African-American counterpart to Princeton. Most of Lincoln's all-white faculty had graduated from Princeton. The two universities shared the same school colors and high academic standards. About half of Lincoln's graduates went on in higher education to study medicine, education, law, and other fields. After receiving his bachelor's degree from Lincoln, Aubrey

Marshall enrolled in medical school and later became a prominent chest surgeon. Norma Marshall hoped that Thurgood would also choose a medical career and become a dentist. She knew that there were very few professional fields open to African-Americans with a college degree. White people generally did not hire black doctors, lawyers, or accountants. As a dentist Thurgood would be able to work in the African-American community and earn a good living. At his mother's urging he enrolled in the predentistry program.

Despite the excellence of Lincoln's curriculum, Marshall's academic career did not get off to a promising start. The future Supreme Court justice preferred playing cards to studying. Like many college freshmen away from home for the first time, he wanted to explore his newfound freedom. He signed up for the Weekend Club, a group of fun-seeking students who vowed to find off-campus adventure to fill every weekend. In his sophomore year he joined a boisterous fraternity. His sociability and sense of humor won him many friends.

At Lincoln Marshall encountered students from distant parts of the world and every economic background. For the first time in his life he met young men from countries in Africa, several of whom wore the splendid robes and striking jewelry of their homelands. He went to classes alongside two future presidents of African nations: Kwame Nkrumah of Ghana and Nnamdi Azikiwe of Nigeria. The American students were equally interesting. One of them, Langston Hughes, later earned a reputation as one of the finest writers of our time. He published his first book of poetry the year he entered Lincoln. Another student,

Cabell "Cab" Calloway, went on to become one of America's great bandleaders.

Since he was smart, Marshall sailed through the first couple of years at college "without exactly killing myself," as he said in a letter to his father. Unfortunately he also sailed right into a suspension from school. One night he and his fraternity friends got carried away and shaved the hair off the fraternity's freshmen recruits. This activity was one example of funny and sometimes dangerous tricks older fraternity members played on the younger students who wanted to join. The practice, called hazing, is banned in many schools and was outlawed at Lincoln. Caught in the act by school officials, Marshall was sent home for months. The suspension cured Marshall of his wild behavior. "I got the horsin' around out of my system," he said later.

Marshall's restlessness was partially due to his boredom with dentistry. Reading textbooks on how to extract teeth and cure gum disease made him realize that, unlike his brother, Aubrey, he was not cut out for the medical profession. Fortunately his interest in interacting with people led him into debating, an activity that paved the way for his career as a lawyer. From the day he signed up for the debating club, on a hunch that he would enjoy it, to the time of his graduation, Marshall excelled in the art of arguing, becoming the club's star member. He spent hours preparing speeches and doing research on the facts and arguments that would outwit his opponents. "If I were taking debating for credit," he wrote home, "I would be the biggest honor student they ever had around here." Over six feet tall and weighing close to two hundred pounds, the brilliant orator was an intimidating opponent. His teammates referred to him as Wrathful Marshall because of his aggressive style. Wrathful led his club to a spate of victories and prizes.

Marshall's power of persuasion was put to memorable use one Friday night on the eve of Lincoln's big football game. During a pep rally for the college's lackluster team, Marshall leapt up on the auditorium stage and delivered a twenty-minute morale booster. The audience cheered him on with shouts and applause. The pep talk had its effect, for the next day Lincoln's team, known to lose a game by as much as sixty points, tied its opponent in the big match.

On another evening Marshall got the chance to show off his fighting spirit in an area that touched him on a deeper level—segregated movie theaters. Shortly before Christmas break, as the bleary-eyed student was plodding through dentistry textbooks in his dormitory room, his friend, John Little, barged in to propose a scheme concocted by Little and the other students at Lincoln. Little wanted to know if Marshall would join them that night to integrate the local movie house.

Within minutes Marshall was crammed into a Model-T roadster with five other schoolmates on his way to Oxford. As the car bounced along, they sang. At the theater Marshall's friend, Cran Harewood, strolled up to the woman behind the ticket window to buy six seats. When she handed over the tickets, she told Harewood that the group would have to sit in the balcony with other black ticketholders because of "house rules." As they trudged into the theater, prepared to ignore the house rules, Marshall saw three more groups of Lincoln students making their way to the ticket window. It was going to be an interesting showdown.

Inside the theater Marshall's group settled into first-floor seats squarely in front of the movie screen. They were followed by twenty more Lincoln students, who did the same. Within a few minutes a young usher came up to the group and whispered that they would have to move to the balcony. The Lincoln students ignored him. Then a more threatening voice was heard. Thurgood pricked up his ears to angry words coming from a man behind him: "Nigger, why don't you-all just get out of here and go sit where you belong?" Thurgood felt the blood rush to his face. He later wrote his parents what he experienced on hearing those words: "You can't really tell what that kind of person looks like because it's just an ugly *feeling* that's looking at you, not a real face." Nevertheless Thurgood held back from punching the man as he would have done as a high school student. Instead he calmly told the intruder, "My name is Marshall, and I paid for my ticket and I intend to sit wherever I please." The white man snarled, "I don't take no lip from any punk nigger." Restraining his anger again, Marshall replied, "That's very interesting. If I see such a person, I'll be sure to tell him what you said. Now, why don't you leave?"

Surprisingly the students didn't hear from either the usher or the white man again, and they spent the remainder of their time in the theater absorbed in the cowboy Western film on screen. They were lucky, though. In other circumstances they might have ended up in jail for disturbing the peace. Marshall figured the chances of that happening in Oxford were slim. As he wrote to his father, "We found out that they only had one fat cop in the whole town and they wouldn't have had the nerve or the room in the jail to arrest all of us."

Scary as it was to stand up to the whites in the theater, the students had won important ground in doing so. Instead of fighting back, the whites chose to ignore them. Thurgood wrote to his parents about how that felt, saying, "But the amazing thing was when we were leaving . . . all those other [white] people . . . didn't even look at us—at least as far as I know. I'm not sure I like being invisible, but maybe it's better than being put to shame and not able to respect yourself." Thanks to Marshall and the others, Lincoln students from that night forward sat wherever they wished in Oxford's movie theater. Thurgood remembered the incident as one of the happiest in his life.

The college student's travels with his friends during his junior year brought him another happy experience, this one on the emotional front. During one of his many weekend trips to Philadelphia, Marshall joined other Lincoln students at a social event sponsored by the Cherry Street Memorial Church. Their motives were not entirely religious. As Marshall joked later, "We went in there because we learned that's where all the cute chicks went." The "cute chick" he met that day was Vivian Burey, a smart coed studying education at the University of Pennsylvania. She soon married Marshall and remained his wife until the day she died.

After meeting Vivian, Marshall spent every free moment shuttling back and forth between Oxford and Philadelphia to be with her. The two grew eager to get married. "First we decided to get married five years after I graduated, then three, then one, and we finally did just before I started my last semester.'' Knowing that the young couple would find it hard to support themselves financially during Marshall's senior year of college, both sets of parents urged them to postpone the marriage until their job prospects were better. But Thurgood and Vivian were too impatient to wait. After much pleading, they won their parents' approval. The wedding took place on September 4, 1929, almost two months before a stock market crash hurled the country into the worst depression it has ever known. The new Mr. and Mrs. Thurgood Marshall were only twenty-one years old.

As predicted, Thurgood and Vivian Marshall had trouble making ends meet during their first years together. After moving into a small apartment in Oxford, Vivian Marshall worked as a secretary while her husband balanced schoolwork and a succession of jobs that included bellhop, grocery clerk, and waiter. The lack of sleep and lean times did not seem to intrude on their happiness, however. Marshall proudly introduced Vivian—nicknamed Buster—Marshall to all his friends and professors. She, in turn, provided him with love and stability. Said one observer, "She helped turn him around and inspired in him an academic zeal.''

Marshall's married life gave him a new enthusiasm for his schoolwork as well as time to study and read. He delved into the works of African-American writers who were part of a new movement called the Harlem Renaissance. This important cultural rebirth originated among the artists, writers, intellectuals, and musicians of New York City's Harlem district, and it influenced American culture for generations. The

25

writers most admired during Marshall's university years were Jean Toomer, Countee Cullen, Claude McKay, Langston Hughes, and Zora Neale Hurston.

In addition to reading works of the latest African-American authors, Marshall studied the writings of the established scholar and civil rights crusader W. E. B. Du Bois. Du Bois's essays, published in *The Souls of Black Folk* in 1903, presented a disturbing picture of the mistreatment of blacks in America. Later he published a follow-up collection, *The Gift of Black Folk*. Du Bois believed that higher education was the key vehicle African-Americans could use to pull themselves up to a position of equality. He urged African-Americans to band together to end segregation in schools.

Marshall was moved by the essays, but he found Du Bois's affiliation with the National Association for the Advancement of Colored People (NAACP) equally intriguing. Founded in 1909, following the racial incident that occurred during the summer of Marshall's birth, the NAACP, along with the Urban League, was the leading organization fighting for the rights of African-Americans. Serving as the organization's director of publications and research, Du Bois edited the NAACP-sponsored periodical *The Crisis*. Each issue reached a broad audience with its outspoken views, poems, essays, short stories, and news reports on topics of pressing concern to African-Americans. Every month *The Crisis* tallied the number of lynchings that took place around the nation. Because of its celebrated magazine and court fights against discrimination, the NAACP spread its influence far and wide.

The most publicized court battle fought by the NAACP had occurred in 1923, when Thurgood was fifteen years old. The case revolved around a group of poor, black Arkansas sharecroppers who staged a revolt to secure better treatment. In the decades after the Civil War destitute laborers of all races worked farmland for large landowners in return for a meager share of the crops. Given little food and treated badly, most sharecroppers endured slaverylike conditions. When the sharecroppers banded together to organize a peaceful protest, whites in the area fired guns at them and combed the countryside in a violent rampage against blacks. As a result of the disturbance seventy-nine blacks were arrested and brought to trial in front of an armed mob. Within one hour an all-white jury sentenced twelve men to death by hanging and sixty-seven more to prison terms.

When the NAACP took on the case, it hired a brilliant black attorney from Arkansas. The attorney, Scipio Africanus Jones, did a masterful job, getting six of the convictions withdrawn in Arkansas's highest court. Trying to get the rest of the convictions thrown out, NAACP lawyers brought the case to the U.S. Supreme Court. The plight of the sharecroppers received national attention, and African-Americans anxiously awaited the outcome of the trial. Vivian Marshall recalled that on the day the Supreme Court verdict was announced, her father and six friends huddled around the big wooden radio in their living room to listen to the news. They were elated when it came: the Supreme Court reversed the convictions. Eventually every one of the poor farmers was set free. It was a stunning victory for African-Americans everywhere.

The Arkansas sharecroppers case was the NAACP's most famous during its early years, but under the direction of Arthur B. Spingarn, the organization won victories in such important areas as voting rights, equal housing, and trial procedure. Their triumphs laid the legal foundation for many of Marshall's victories later on. The NAACP's strong record bolstered Marshall's faith in the legal process as a means of social reform.

Ideas about the legal process and social reform were uppermost in the Lincoln student's mind now that he was a senior. As graduation neared, it was time for him to consider what to do with his life. Dentistry was out of the question. An F he received in an important biology course made continuing in the field difficult. Besides, the subject continued to bore him. After discussing his future with Vivian and his parents, Marshall decided to pursue the study of law. In order to get a law degree, he would need to complete three more years of school. He also had to find a law school with an excellent reputation. A lawyer's training and academic credentials could make or break a career.

Marshall's grades from Lincoln presented no obstacle to attending the law school of his choice, but the same couldn't be said about the color of his skin. Because of its convenient location in Baltimore and its excellent reputation, the University of Maryland Law School was Marshall's first choice. Unfortunately the all-white institution had an ironclad policy: No blacks need apply. Shut out of the University of Maryland, Marshall opted to go to Howard University, the venerated black university located in Washington, D.C.

In choosing Howard, Marshall selected the best place in the country to learn about civil rights law. Founded in 1867 to educate the newly freed African-Americans, Howard had always championed an equal role for blacks in society. In the late 1920s, however, Howard got its first black president, Mordecai Johnson, who turned the school into a training ground for future civil rights activists. Within a few short years he had built its first law school designed "to train men to get the constitutional rights of our people."

Accepted at Howard and eager to begin law studies, Marshall completed his final year at Lincoln in June 1930, receiving his A.B. degree with honors in humanities. Following a shaky start, Marshall had proved to be a top-notch student. After graduation he and Buster moved in with his parents in Baltimore so that they could save every extra dollar for law school. The young couple was lucky to find such a comfortable home. The Depression had sent many less fortunate people to the streets to scrounge for handouts of food and shelter. Still, Marshall's parents were not well off. To help pay for her son's education, Norma Marshall sold her wedding ring. It was a sacrifice she would never regret.

4

A Legal Whiz

THURGOOD MARSHALL ENTERED Howard University Law School in 1930, poor but determined. He got up every morning at five-thirty to catch the early train to Washington, where his classes were held. Back in Baltimore by late afternoon, he reported to his part-time job and then studied after dinner well into the night. "I got through simply by overwhelming the job," he recalled later. "I was at it twenty hours a day, seven days a week." The twenty-hour days took their toll, though. During his law school years Marshall lost forty pounds.

Despite the rugged schedule, Marshall trained for his new career with the enthusiasm of an Olympics-bound athlete. Within several days of classes Marshall realized, "This was it. This was what I wanted to do for as long as I lived." He became so engrossed in his law studies that by the end of his first year he was the top student in his class. The honor brought him a good-paying job in Howard's law library, but also kept him in Washington until ten o'clock at night.

Not one to give up his social life under pressure of work, Marshall acquired a large circle of friends at

Howard and found the time to squeeze in his favorite card games. A fellow law student recalled that Marshall "was happy-go-lucky on the face of it, but he managed to get quite a lot of work done when nobody was looking." Marshall's easygoing manner offset his new seriousness about the direction his life was taking. To complete school requirements, he enrolled in courses in business, labor, criminal justice, and other branches of law. In his senior year he concentrated in corporate law, knowing that it would help him in his private law practice later on. As an attorney he wanted to handle disputes between workers and management. Yet the subject that consumed his interest was civil rights, the study of basic privileges guaranteed to all U.S. citizens in the Constitution.

Marshall knew these rights by heart. After all, he had memorized the Constitution as an unruly adolescent. Having grown up under segregation's iron rule, Marshall knew that the rights spelled out in the Constitution did not always translate into everyday life. The United States had a long history of separating theory from practice.

That separation went way back to the days when the United States was founded on the principle "All men are created equal." The phrase, embedded in the Declaration of Independence, was also the foundation for the freedoms guaranteed in the U.S. Constitution, the first ten of which are known as the Bill of Rights. Yet throughout the first hundred years of U.S. history, slavery belied the ideal of equality. It wasn't until the mid-twentieth century that the Supreme Court stepped in to uphold the equal rights for all citizens promised in the Constitution. Before that time its decisions reinforced the unequal status quo. After the

31

Civil War the Court bowed to the South's wishes in striking down civil rights legislation while upholding segregation. Later, with prodding from the NAACP and other reformist groups, the Court changed many of its ideas about the meaning of rights guaranteed in the Constitution. It struck down unfair practices in housing, voting procedure, courtroom trials, and other important areas.

African-Americans weren't the only group to be left out of the "all men are created equal" ideal, though they were given the roughest treatment in the republic's early years. Women and some minorities also suffered discrimination. It wasn't until 1920, for instance, that women got the right to vote—well after black males were guaranteed the same privilege. Only after years of pressure from women's rights groups did lawmakers guarantee their right to vote in the Nineteenth Amendment. In studying these and other civil rights struggles, Marshall came to the conclusion that the United States Constitution is one of the most remarkable documents of freedom in the world. But he also realized that its words must be continually challenged and revitalized to reflect changing ideas about fairness. Marshall came to view the Constitution as a living document, open to interpretation. If it had remained stuck in the context of the times in which it was first written, he reasoned, blacks and women would not have such guarantees as the right to vote. In this line of reasoning, the young law student followed the thinking of the great justice John Marshall, one of the earliest members of the Supreme Court. Thurgood also came to the conclusion that, as chief watchdog of the rights guaranteed in the Constitution, the Supreme Court had a responsibility to interpret those rights in light of modern-day ideas and circumstances.

Marshall's new ideas about fairness and the lawful means of securing it were shaped by his outstanding professors at Howard. No group of African-American legal scholars was readier than they to breathe new life into the Constitution. Handpicked by President Mordecai Johnson, Marshall's professors brought such high standards to Howard that within a few years of their arrival the law school became the first all-black law school to be accredited (approved) by the American Bar Association, the most prestigious organization of lawyers.

This new crop of professors made stringent demands on the students. Toughest among them was Charles Hamilton Houston, dubbed Iron Shoes and Cement Pants by Marshall and the other students. Of the thirty people who signed up for his class, only eight or ten managed to get through it. Fortunately Marshall was one of them. Marshall's initial terror of the man gave way to an admiration and friendship lasting many years. "What Charlie beat into our heads," Marshall recalled later, "was excellence."

Excellence marked every step of Houston's career. One of the first black students admitted to Harvard Law School, the tough-minded legal scholar graduated at the top of his class. He then became an outstanding lawyer before being hired as vice-dean of Howard Law School. He devoted his life to the cause of civil rights, and his law cases paved the way for *Brown v. Board of Education* and other landmarks in desegregation. The dedicated man put in eighteen- to

33

twenty-hour days, and he expected those who worked with him to do the same. His intense work habits quickly rubbed off on Marshall.

During the many cases he took on for the NAACP, Houston came to realize the importance of a well-prepared and well-argued case. If a black lawyer wanted respect, he had to earn it the hard way. Marshall later talked about Houston's views on the matter: "He used to tell us that doctors could bury their mistakes, but lawyers couldn't. And he'd drive home to us that we would be competing, not only with white lawyers but with really well-trained white lawyers, so there wasn't any point in crying in our beer about being Negroes."*

Houston demanded high standards from his students because he wanted them to go out in the world and make a difference as social reformers. Marshall said later, "Harvard was training people to join big law firms; Howard was teaching lawyers to go to court. Charlie's phrase was Social Engineer. He wanted us to be part of the community. He wanted the lawyer to take over leadership in the community." One of Houston's favorite mottoes was "Freedom that is built on law is the only kind that will last—and the only kind worth having." Those words guided Marshall through the toughest times of his life.

Under Houston's tutelage Marshall saw his new career taking shape. He grew to idolize "Charlie" and in turn became the professor's prize pupil. Because of this favored status Marshall was invited to join Hous-

---

*To describe African-Americans, Marshall employed the term *Negroes*, in wide use at the time. In 1989 he switched to the contemporary term *Afro-Americans*.

ton and other Howard professors at NAACP legal meetings. There he watched lawyers discuss important civil rights cases and plan strategy for upcoming trials. For the meetings, which lasted well into the night, the enthusiastic law student lent a hand in everything from legal research to rustling up coffee and sandwiches. A talented debater, Marshall often plunged into the discussions. His boldness impressed NAACP chief executive Walter White, who remembered Marshall in those days as a "lanky, brash, young senior law student. . . . I used to wonder at his presence and sometimes was amazed at his assertiveness in challenging positions [taken] by Charlie and the other lawyers."

Houston wasn't Marshall's only mentor. Another brilliant professor who taught him a lot was William Henry Hastie. A Harvard Law School graduate who went on to become the nation's first black federal judge, Hastie, like Houston, was an active member of the NAACP. He got his students to research and discuss important civil rights cases of the day. When Marshall was only a second-year law student, Hastie gave him the opportunity to work on a legal case deciding an issue close to Marshall's heart—desegregation. The case arose when a black college graduate, denied admission to the University of North Carolina Law School because of his race, decided to sue the university. Unfortunately he lost his case, but he was so determined to secure his rights that he asked Hastie to take his case to a federal court for an appeal, or review, of the decision. A federal court that reviews the legality of decisions made by lower courts is called a federal court of appeals.

Hastie put Marshall to work on a team researching

every aspect of the Fourteenth Amendment as it related to segregation in schools. Their job was to write a brief, which is a summary of all the arguments supporting one side's position. The team was supposed to argue that the University of North Carolina violated the student's right to equal protection of the laws under the Fourteenth Amendment.

Still chafing from his own exclusion from the University of Maryland Law School a couple of years earlier, Marshall threw himself into the job with the zeal of a reformer. He spent long hours in the law library poring over books on the background of segregation. He found out that segregation was practiced on a limited basis before the Civil War, but it wasn't until after the war that separation of whites and blacks hardened into law. In that hardening process it was the Supreme Court, not Congress, that had played a decisive role. Just after 1865, when the Civil War ended, Congress spent nine difficult years passing the first civil rights legislation in U.S. history. The laws were intended to give teeth to the Thirteenth, Fourteenth, and Fifteenth amendments to the Constitution, passed after the Civil War over the objections of the Southern states. The Thirteenth Amendment abolished slavery and the Fifteenth spelled out voting rights for black males.

The Fourteenth Amendment, adopted in 1868, proved far more problematical. It allowed citizenship for blacks and gave them equal rights. Its first clause stated, "No State . . . shall deny to any person within its jurisdiction equal protection of the laws." Yet its clear mandate for equal rights quickly got lost in the shuffle of postwar politics. Almost immediately the effect of the Fourteenth Amendment was eroded by the fact that the Southern states had been forced to sign it and other amendments as a condition of their reentry into the Union.

Adding to the problem of Southern hostility was the fact that the wording of the amendment left an important loophole for those who wished to undermine it. The amendment said that no *state* could deny a person equal protection of the laws. But what about an individual? Could one citizen in a state deny another citizen equal protection of the laws and get away with it? Many people said yes. From the day of its passage in Congress, presidents, politicians, lawyers, historians, and reformers have grappled with the meaning of the Fourteenth Amendment. Depending on interpretation, it either supports or destroys the legal foundation on which segregation rests.

In 1883 the Supreme Court dealt the amendment a serious blow. It declared that the U.S. government could prevent *states* from denying its citizens equal rights, but it could not prevent *individuals* from doing the same. In one fell swoop it rendered the civil rights legislation null and void and crippled the Fourteenth Amendment for decades. Hearing the Supreme Court's decision in 1883, Frederick Douglass commented bitterly, "The future historian will turn to the year 1883 to find the most flagrant example of national deterioration. Here he will find the Supreme Court of the nation . . . nullifying the Fourteenth Amendment, and placing itself on the side of prejudice, proscription, and persecution."

Given encouragement by the Supreme Court, lawmakers everywhere enacted segregation laws that forced African-Americans into separate and inferior schools, trains, houses, and just about every facility that could be separated. At the same time lynchings multiplied, and blacks withdrew in record numbers from political office. It was in this climate of fear and reprisal that Homer Adolph Plessy, "one-eighth Negro and seven-eighths white" decided to challenge Louisiana's segregation laws. Refusing to move to the "colored only" car of a railroad train traveling from New Orleans to Covington, Plessy placed himself in the white section, and got arrested. Plessy's lawyers brought his case to trial, and eventually to the Supreme Court, where they hoped to win the first of many antisegregation victories.

Unfortunately they miscalculated. The Supreme Court was swept up in the fashionable theories of the day that denounced federal meddling in the affairs of states and individuals. Just a few years earlier, in a case similar to Plessy's, the Court had ruled that a state could allow segregation on its railroad trains. In Plessy's case it went further, adjudicating the greatest setback to civil rights since slavery. In *Plessy v. Ferguson* the justices ruled that "legislation is powerless to eradicate racial instincts." They went on to lay down the foundations for the "separate but equal" doctrine that justified segregation for the next fifty-eight years.

In reviewing the Supreme Court's ruling in *Plessy*, Marshall and the other students thought they found their saving argument for the North Carolina case. "Separate but equal" means that blacks and whites may be accorded separate facilities, but they had to be equal. Clearly the University of North Carolina had not provided the black applicant with an equal alternative school after rejecting him! When the students finished writing the brief, they sought approval from

Hastie, who took it with him to the North Carolina Court of Appeals. But in its decision the court of appeals gave him the same arguments the Supreme Court had used back in 1883. It ruled that the University of North Carolina was essentially a private institution and therefore not subject to regulation by the Fourteenth Amendment. Once again a black man was told by the courts that the Fourteenth Amendment did not protect him.

Though he lost that round, Marshall learned a valuable lesson: If he was going to help topple Jim Crow from his mighty perch, he was going to have to get hold of a lot more experience and legal ammunition. With that goal in mind, Marshall spent the next couple of years working so hard that he graduated first in his class, with honors. He was proud of his success, but even more grateful to Howard for giving him the hands-on experience he needed. After finishing his degree at Howard he never forgot the lessons he had learned from his professors, and he credited the tough standards of the school with much of his success. Giving tips on success to an assembly of Howard students many years later, he echoed the words of Charles Houston: "When you get in a courtroom . . . you are in competition with a well-trained white lawyer and you'd better be at least as good as he is; and if you expect to win, you'd better be better. If I give you five cases to read overnight, you'd better read eight. And when I say eight, you read ten. You go that step further, and you might make it."

Marshall now had to take that "step further" on his own. Impatient to open his law practice, he turned down a postgraduate scholarship to Harvard. To start his practice, Marshall had to take the Maryland bar examination (the test on state law he had to pass in order to be certified) and to find enough money to open shop. The first part was easy—he passed the bar with high marks. The second, though, proved to be more difficult. It was 1933, and the Great Depression had hit rock bottom. Businesses that had flourished in the 1920s slowly went bankrupt. Over half the black population was out of work. As charity bread lines lengthened and soup kitchens overflowed with starving people, President Roosevelt set up emergency relief measures. Eventually Roosevelt's measures worked, but in 1933 Marshall's prospects for opening a new business catering to the black community couldn't have been worse.

Adding to Marshall's economic problems was the fact that black lawyers faced a wall of prejudice. Few white clients would hire them, and black clients with money tended to hire whites. They had good reasons for doing so. A white lawyer was more likely to win cases argued in front of all-white juries and judges. In 1933 few African-Americans got hired as jurors or judges. At the time Marshall set up practice there were fewer than a dozen black lawyers in the city of Baltimore. It would take many years for women, blacks, and minorities to break into the legal system.

Undaunted by the odds against him, Marshall hired a secretary and opened a one-room attorney's office at 48 Redwood Street in east Baltimore. To supplement his meager furnishings, Marshall's mother donated the rug from her living room floor. For the first year Marshall's list of clients was as empty as his office. The few needy people who did enter his doors could not afford to pay his moderate fees. Marshall never turned them away. Instead he showed a soft heart and what one secretary described as "a genius for ignoring cases that might earn him any money." At the end of twelve months he showed a loss, after expenses, of one thousand dollars. Marshall later described how he scraped through the lean times: "One day I'd bring two lunches and the next day my secretary would bring two lunches and sometimes we'd be the only two people in that office for weeks at a time."

The less-fortunate members of society brought him their problems with evictions, bad landlords, police brutality, and other legal matters. Arguing their cases in court, Marshall developed his characteristic style—respectful of the judge, but forceful in pressing the cause of justice. One observer who was impressed by Marshall's courtroom presence was the renowned writer Langston Hughes. He remarked that Marshall "moved many a judge to search his conscience and come up with decisions he probably did not know he had in him." Avoiding complicated legal jargon, Marshall went right for the heart of an argument in clear, everyday language. Yet at the same time he worked hard to avoid having his simple language mistaken for simplemindedness. Marshall was stunned one day when he overheard a Baltimore court clerk refer to a black lawyer's written arguments as a "nigger brief." He vowed that his work would never be evaluated with such racist contempt. True to his training under Houston, he meticulously prepared each case, no matter how small or insignificant.

Eventually word of Marshall's legal prowess spread, netting him several big clients. Among them were a Baltimore laundry company, labor organizations, building associations, corporations, and a wealthy man named Carl Murphy, whose generosity brought Marshall once again into the unpaid service of the NAACP. Scion of Baltimore's leading black family and publisher of the *Afro-American* weekly, Murphy donated a large sum of money to revive the local chapter of the NAACP. He asked Marshall to become the chapter's attorney. Marshall agreed, and took on the NAACP work during the hours off from his private practice.

Spearheading the effort to resuscitate the Baltimore NAACP was Lillie Jackson, a tough and energetic housewife who worked with Marshall to rally support in the African-American neighborhoods. Marshall traveled from one community to another, delivering speeches that attempted to break through the lethargy he noticed everywhere. According to the Reverend A. J. Payne, leader of the Baptist church in Baltimore, his audiences responded. "Young Marshall . . . showed his courage and tenacity," Payne recalled, "and the people liked him, the common people and the professional people both. . . . He'd say that, Jim Crow or no Jim Crow, we were free citizens and as such we had rights, but we were going to have to fight to get them. People in the community looked up to him."

"In those days Thurgood was lean, hard, and Hollywood handsome," Roy Wilkins recalled. Wilkins was an executive at the NAACP national headquarters in New York. When the Baltimore branch got established, Wilkins was invited down to give a speech. He remembered Marshall as smooth-mannered on the outside and tough as nails on the inside. "[Marshall] wore natty, double-breasted suits with immaculate white handkerchiefs sticking out of the breast pocket;

he had a neatly trimmed mustache and a way of wrinkling his brow that made him look like a skeptical house detective listening to the alibi of a philandering [unfaithful] husband.'' Wilkins went on to note that "his tactics combined a shrewd Southern way of leaving white foes enough rope to hang themselves with a Northern spare-me-the-sorghum style.''

Wilkins also got to know Marshall's affable, easygoing side. After the New York executive gave his speech, he and Marshall went out for drinks. Their conversation lasted half the night. When the deeply religious Mrs. Jackson heard about their drinking and staying up late, she was incensed. She fired off an angry note to Wilkins's boss in New York asking that the young Wilkins refrain from corrupting Baltimore in the future. Fortunately Wilkins was amused, and in the many trips he made to Baltimore from that day forward his friendship and admiration for the woman grew.

Marshall kicked off his new role as NAACP attorney with a boycott of Baltimore stores that refused to hire blacks. Targeting the stores along Pennsylvania Avenue, Marshall and his colleagues organized picket lines along the storefronts. Manning the lines were unemployed African-American high school students. They urged shoppers to stay away from the stores until the white managers hired blacks. The plan worked well. Hurting from the drop in sales, the store owners grouped together to sue the NAACP for hurting business. Marshall now had an important case on his hands.

Joining Marshall in defending the NAACP was his former professor, Charles Houston. Marshall wrote the brief for the case, and Houston argued it before the court. As a team they were unbeatable. The judge not only ruled in their favor but congratulated them on their outstanding work. In that memorable case the two civil rights advocates scored a victory for public protest and freedom of speech. Within a year they would crack the barricades of all-white graduate schools.

In the meanwhile, though, Marshall had a score to settle. During all the years Marshall's mother taught school in Baltimore, she got paid less money than her white colleagues received for the same work. In Maryland a grammar school teacher was likely to earn $600 a year if he or she was black, and $1,100 if white. Like nearly every black teacher in Maryland and throughout the South, Mrs. Marshall was a victim of job discrimination.

Marshall and Mrs. Jackson decided it was time to correct this unfair practice. Joining an NAACP campaign, they helped organize educators throughout the state to sue their school boards for equal pay. Since many of the teachers were afraid of losing their jobs during the protest, the NAACP raised money for an emergency fund to make up for lost salaries. After several years the equal-pay drive met with success. For the first time in history, teachers and administrators of both races received matching salaries. The first administrator to benefit from the campaign was William Gibbs, a school principal who saw his salary more than double, from $612 to $1,475 a year.

No one was more proud of this achievement than Mrs. Marshall. Just a few years earlier she had given up her wedding ring to finance her son's education. Now she had the satisfaction of seeing him make a real difference in the world.

5

"The Time Is Ripe"

ONE DAY, WHILE Marshall was working in his law office, a shy, clean-cut African-American walked in and introduced himself as Donald Gaines Murray. The student told Marshall he had just graduated from Amherst College in Massachusetts and he wanted to pursue his graduate study at the all-white University of Maryland Law School. Marshall was impressed by Murray's determination. Like Marshall, Murray had grown up in Baltimore and gone to Frederick Douglass High School. They both had set out as young men to practice law in their home city. But there Marshall hoped the similarities between the two would end. Marshall never got the chance to go to the University of Maryland and he hoped matters would turn out differently for Murray.

Keen to challenge the university's stand on segregation, Marshall agreed to take Murray's case, and immediately got on the phone to Charles Houston in New York. He and Houston mapped out an argument based on the NAACP's new plan for desegregation. The plan, worked out by Houston and his colleague, Nathan Margold, called for an assault on all-white Southern graduate schools. They called this area of education the "soft underbelly" of segregation because it was the easiest legal target. Discrimination against black candidates was a lot more obvious at the graduate-school level than at the elementary or high school level. Whereas public schools took in students from the local neighborhoods, graduate schools catered to students from across the country. A qualified black candidate denied admission to an all-white university was clearly the victim of deliberate discrimination, not neighborhood zoning. The second reason the NAACP staff targeted graduate schools was because Southerners appeared less hostile to integration at the upper levels of education than at the grade-school level.

Houston and Marshall thought they had found the perfect integration candidate in Donald Murray. He was smart, qualified, and determined to study Maryland law. The University of Maryland, however, had been swayed by none of these qualifications. After rejecting Murray because of his race, they offered him a no-win choice: He could either accept their scholarship to study at an out-of-state law school or he could attend Princess Anne Academy, a segregated school in Maryland that offered no law degree. Murray refused both options. When he reapplied to the university, he was told by its president, Raymond A. Pearson, "The University does not accept Negro students." It was then that Murray decided to sue.

When *Murray v. Pearson* reached the Baltimore court in June 1935, Marshall was nervous about arguing his first big school case. Giving him moral support were Norma, William, and Buster Marshall, who observed the proceedings from the visitors section. During the four days of the trial Marshall and Houston took turns arguing the points laid out in Marshall's meticulously constructed brief. In his closing statements, Marshall told the court that the "equal" portion of the "separate but equal" doctrine was being tested here for the first time. The University of Maryland, he argued, had to provide Murray with an education in law equal to the one provided to its white students. If the institution could not provide him with such an education outside of its walls, then it had to let Murray in.

To everyone's amazement the court agreed. The judge ordered the university to admit Murray, the first black in its history. Marshall listened calmly to the ground-breaking verdict. Not wanting to break his composure in front of the judge, he walked slowly out of the courtroom to join his family. Then, when he got to the hall, he burst forth in excitement. After hugging his parents, he whirled Buster around in an exuberant tango. Later, celebrating the victory at lunch with Houston and his family, Marshall quipped, "As of today, we are in the education business!"

Murray was no less exuberant. The following fall he enrolled in the law school, where he was welcomed by students and professors alike. After getting his law degree three years later he set up private practice in Baltimore. For the rest of his career he showed his gratitude to the NAACP by providing them with free legal services. Seeing Murray get in to the University of Maryland gave Marshall deep satisfaction. One reporter covering the trial called the verdict "sweet revenge" for Marshall and asked the lawyer how he felt about it. "Wonderful," Marshall replied. "I enjoyed it to no end."

Shortly after the Murray case Marshall received a

phone call from Charles Houston asking him to be his assistant at the NAACP in New York. Houston informed him that the job, which required travel in the South, would be both frustrating and dangerous. He also joked that Marshall had a chance of becoming the next Scipio Africanus Jones, the lawyer who defended Arkansas sharecroppers back in the 1920s. Marshall responded with his own quip. On hearing that the salary was $2,400 a year, he said, "I always tell my wife that the best civil rights lawyer is the poorest man in town." Though Marshall accepted the post, he decided not to abandon his clients in Baltimore. Instead, he moved his practice into a room in his family's house and commuted between the two cities.

The assistant special counsel and his new boss teamed up in Marshall's beat-up '29 Ford and began the first of many sojourns in the South. They drove from town to town, gathering information, planning strategies, and filing antidiscrimination lawsuits in the courts. The Deep South was a new experience for Marshall, who had never lived in a place where a slur to a white person could cost him his life. The two men kept a very low profile. Since they were not allowed in most decent hotels, they slept in friends' houses and ate in their car, which also served as their office. Marshall marveled at how hard Houston worked. "Charlie would sit in my car . . . and type out briefs," he recalled. "And he could type up a storm—faster than any secretary—and not just with two fingers going. I mean he used 'em all."

One day the two civil rights attorneys got a chance to test the "soft underbelly" of Missouri's educational system. Like Donald Murray in Maryland, a young African-American named Lloyd Gaines was denied admission to the University of Missouri Law School. The university offered him free tuition at another school, but it was out of state. Instead of accepting the offer, Gaines sued the university. His case, *Gaines v. Missouri*, worked its way up through the state and federal court system. Houston and Marshall hoped to bring it to the Supreme Court, where it would be the first school-segregation case to reach the highest court in the nation. The chances of any case reaching the Supreme Court are slim. The Court receives thousands of requests for hearings each year and elects to act on only a small portion of them. In order to qualify for review, the cases must raise important constitutional issues.

Fortunately the Supreme Court agreed that *Gaines v. Missouri* was worthy of review and scheduled a hearing. Marshall's nervousness at preparing his first Supreme Court case was compounded by the fact that the future course of school desegregation hung in the balance. He spent many hours working on the brief that Houston and two other NAACP attorneys relied on to argue the case. Once again, the young attorney called upon the Fourteenth Amendment, demanding that the University of Missouri either provide separate and equal facilities for Gaines or admit him to the university. On December 12, 1938, the Court handed down its favorable decision, forcing the University of Missouri to open its doors. It was a resounding triumph for Gaines and African-American students everywhere.

Gaines was the last major victory Marshall shared with his boss and mentor. In late 1938 Houston resigned from his full-time post at the NAACP and handed over the reins of power to Marshall, now thirty years old. Though Houston moved to Washington, D.C., to work at his private law practice, he continued to fight for equal rights and offered his services in many NAACP-sponsored cases. Filling Houston's post as special counsel demanded that Thurgood and Buster Marshall close up shop in Baltimore and move to New York. The small increase in salary gave them just enough money to rent a walk-up apartment in Harlem, the African-American business and cultural center located at the northern tip of Manhattan. From there Marshall commuted to the NAACP's downtown headquarters on lower Fifth Avenue.

At first Marshall found the NAACP offices too formal and stuffy—"tush-tush," he called them. He joked that the executives were referred to as "Dr. Whoosis" and "Mr. Whatsis." They came to work in suits and ties and maintained a strict pecking order. Within a few weeks of his arrival the down-to-earth boss got rid of "nonsense like that, bowing and scraping like an embassy scene." Marshall worked in his rolled-up shirtsleeves, ate deli sandwiches with his staff, and had everybody calling each other by first names. "Thurgood was always one of the gang," an aide recalled. "He never put barriers between himself and the less exalted."

In October 1939 the NAACP set up a nonprofit organization called the Legal Defense and Education Fund, known simply as Fund, Inc., or the Inc. Fund. Marshall was appointed its director. A nonprofit organization dedicated to the cause of equal rights, Fund, Inc., gave free legal advice to African-Americans who suffered racial discrimination. Its main goals were to educate the public about the status of African-Americans in the United States and to help provide them with equal educational opportunities. In its early years the organization targeted discrimination against blacks in legal trials and voting procedure. Eventually Fund, Inc., spearheaded the decades-long school-desegregation drive.

In hiring Marshall as director-counsel of Fund, Inc., NAACP president Walter White recognized the outstanding work performed by the former student-volunteer from Howard University. The young man who had boldly challenged his professors now headed the most important legal-activist organization in the country. Within a few years Marshall directed a staff of ten attorneys and scores of volunteers. He devised legal strategy, prepared and checked briefs, and argued important cases. The work sent him on twenty-three-hour days and continual travel, approximately fifty thousand miles' worth each year. He and his staff combed the nation, bringing antidiscrimination cases to trial in nearly every state. They helped African-Americans exercise their rights to vote, serve on juries, find housing in formerly restricted neighborhoods, and get fair pay.

In the South Marshall ventured into territory as hostile as a black was likely to encounter in the mid-twentieth century. Asked about how he managed to avoid conflict, he said, "I know my way around. I don't go looking for trouble. I ride in the for-colored-only cabs and in the back end of streetcars—quiet as a mouse. I eat in Negro cafés and don't use white washrooms. I don't challenge the customs." Marshall didn't challenge the customs, but they often challenged him. On one trip in Mississippi, he was menaced by a white police officer while waiting for a train. As he recalled later, "this cold-eyed man with a gun on his hip comes

51

up. 'Nigguh,' he said, 'I thought you ought to know the sun ain't nevuh set on a live nigguh in this town.' So I wrapped up my constitutional rights in cellophane, tucked 'em in my hip pocket and got out of sight. And, believe me, I caught the next train out of there."

Instead of wasting his time with small-town bigots, Marshall saved his courage and efforts for worthwhile battles. In one instance his courage took him all the way to the office of Texas's governor. Marshall was incensed by the rough treatment given a black senior citizen asked to serve on a Dallas jury. When the college professor showed up for jury duty, he was told blacks weren't allowed. After lodging a protest, he was thrown out the door and down the courtroom steps. On hearing about the incident, Marshall demanded a conference with Governor James Allred. The governor consented, and after hearing Marshall's argument, he ordered an FBI investigation of the incident and ordered the Texas Rangers to guard the courthouse against further racial violence. In addition Allred announced that no mistreatment of black jurors would be tolerated in the future. Observers of the scene said it was the only time in recent memory that a Southern governor had taken such initiative to protect African-Americans.

Marshall's first Fund, Inc., case to reach the Supreme Court was *Chambers v. Florida*. It dealt with the issue of confessions forced from three men accused of murder. In his brief, Marshall asserted that the men were submitted to nonstop interrogation and had been isolated from lawyers, friends, and family. He said that "sunrise confessions" extracted from the men early in the morning were illegal and could not be used as evidence against them. The Supreme Court justices, who had already ruled forced confessions unconstitutional, agreed with Marshall and overturned the convictions.

Following the *Chambers* case in 1940, the Fund fought three additional lawsuits involving forced confessions. They won the first two, but not the third, *Lyons v. Oklahoma*, a lawsuit that centered around a gruesome murder and confession known as the "Pan of Bones" case. The events of the case were triggered by the murder of a white couple and their child in Hugo, Oklahoma. Shortly after police discovered the family's remains in its burned-down house, they picked up a convenient suspect, handyman W. D. Lyons, who was black. Despite the fact that the police had flimsy evidence to connect Lyons to the murders, they threw him in jail, denied him adequate food and sleep, and periodically beat him. For three weeks he didn't see a lawyer. When Lyons failed to give police the confession they were looking for, they placed a pan of charred and blood-encrusted bones on his lap and told him they were the bones of his victims. The tactic worked. Immediately after seeing the bones and being forced to handle them, Lyons "confessed" to the murders. Police then transferred him to the state penitentiary, where he gave a second confession.

In 1941 Marshall arrived in Hugo, Oklahoma, to prepare for Lyons's trial. The town was at a racial boiling point. Expecting trouble, black citizens had smuggled in weapons to defend themselves. To protect Marshall, they provided him with a bodyguard and a different place to sleep and eat each night. "They scared me more than they comforted me," Marshall confessed later. One night Marshall came face-to-face with a white man who identified himself as the father of the murdered woman. To Marshall's astonishment he offered to testify against the police for their brutal handling of Lyons. By adding the father's testimony to many others he had gathered, Marshall felt sure he could prove Lyons's confession was coerced. He had an unshakable faith in the basic goodness of human nature, noting that "even in the most prejudiced communities, the majority of people have some respect for truth and some sense of justice, no matter how deeply hidden it is at times."

Lyons's trial, however, shook Marshall's faith not only in human nature but also in the legal system. Every police official Marshall brought to the witness stand evaded his questions and conveniently forgot important details. The questioning reached its low point when Marshall showed Sheriff Harmon a picture of the sheriff and a policeman standing next to Lyons, all bruised and bloody. When Marshall asked Sheriff Harmon to identify the wounded man in the photograph, Harmon replied, "These Negroes look nearly alike to me, can't hardly tell them apart." Finally, despite the fact that Marshall got the police to admit that they beat Lyons and used the pan of bones to terrify him, the court found Lyons guilty and sentenced him to life imprisonment. The jury refused to believe that Lyons's confession was coerced.

Marshall then took Lyons's case to the Supreme Court in 1943. He pleaded that Lyons was denied "due process of law" because his confession was forced. The Justices disagreed, ruling that Lyons's second confession at the state penitentiary was not coerced. In doing so, they dealt Marshall his first Supreme Court defeat. As director counsel of Fund, Inc., Marshall argued thirty-two cases before the Supreme Court, and lost four. Yet Marshall's sense of personal defeat was overshadowed by his outrage at what he viewed as the miscarriage of justice that sent Lyons to jail for life.

Aside from legal trials, another area in which Fund, Inc., fought antidiscrimination battles was at the polls. Black voters in many states faced a pattern of discrimination that reached back to Reconstruction days. After the Civil War many whites chose to ignore or sabotage the Fifteenth Amendment that in 1870 gave blacks the right to vote. The stumbling blocks they set up to prevent most blacks from voting lasted in many places until the 1960s.

Prime among these tactics were voting taxes and literacy tests. If a black citizen wanted to vote and could afford to pay the tax, he or she had to pass an exam in reading and writing. To test whites, voting examiners had them complete simple tasks like spelling their names. By contrast, blacks were given complicated questions about U.S. history and subjects that required a high degree of education. Many black candidates were failed for forgetting to dot *is* and cross *ts*. Any African-American who managed to get through the obstacle course was slapped with further restrictions relating to property holding and character assessments. The obstructions did their work. In 1896 Louisiana recorded 130,334 black voters. By 1904 the number had fallen to 1,342. Similar statistics prevailed throughout the South. It wasn't until the voter registration drives of the 1960s that the proportion of black voters climbed.

In the early 1940s there were very few blacks in the South who qualified to vote. Those who did were excluded from casting ballots in the states' most important elections, called primaries. Separate primaries are held by Republican and Democratic parties. They decide which of the party's candidates will run for office in elections. Since for a long time Democrats won nearly every election in the South, the Democratic primaries were all-important. Any citizen of a Southern state who couldn't vote in the primary, for instance, had no voice in deciding who would be governor. Knowing this, white Southerners used various means to make sure blacks couldn't vote in the primaries, including denying them membership in the Democratic party.

Determined to bust open the private club of Democratic politics, Marshall set his sights on what he called "the next milestone on the long road toward political equality." His vehicle was a Texas case brought to the courts by Lonnie Smith, a black citizen who sued the Democratic party for the right to vote in state primaries. The lower courts dismissed Smith's case, saying that the Democratic party was a private institution that could set its own membership rules. With the help of a team of specialists that included his former law professor, William Hastie, Marshall brought *Smith v. Allwright* to the Supreme Court in 1944. The team argued that the right to vote in primaries is guaranteed by the Fifteenth Amendment, which prohibits states from denying citizens the vote "on account of race, color, or previous condition of servitude." The Supreme Court ruled in their favor.

Ruling on an issue, however, is not the same as enforcing it. As a judicial body the Supreme Court has no legislative or enforcement power. It must limit itself to cases brought to its attention. Because they were not codified into law by Congress, the Supreme Court decisions on voting were ignored by many Southern states. Following *Smith v. Allwright*, the governor of South Carolina openly defied the Supreme Court ruling. So Marshall took up the case of a black citizen named George Elmore and sued the state in federal court. In a decision favoring Elmore, Judge J. Waties Waring scolded state officials: "It's time for South Carolina to rejoin the Union," he said. "It's time for South Carolina to fall in step with the other states and adopt the American way of elections." Waring's reprimand pointed up a difficult truth: For many Southerners the Civil War still raged. New battle lines pitted states' rights against human rights.

Eventually white primaries went the way of the stagecoach, disappearing from the landscape of American politics. With another legal obstacle removed, the "long road to political equality" looked shorter and smoother to Marshall in 1944. Despite a few rough spots the legal system was working its way toward providing "equal protection of the laws." Even when the system failed him in these early years, Marshall maintained his optimism. "I never lost faith in my country," he admitted later.

The country he rested his faith in was now embroiled in the bloody battles of World War II. From 1941 to 1945 the United States turned its attention to fighting fascism abroad. During the war many Americans felt that blacks should hold off pressing for their rights. Marshall vehemently disagreed. At the 1944 Wartime Conference of the NAACP he attacked segregation in housing, transportation, jobs, and public facilities. He closed his speech by saying, "We must not be delayed by people who say 'the time is not ripe,' nor should we proceed with caution for fear of destroying the 'status quo.' Persons who deny to us our civil rights should be brought to justice now. Many people believe the time is always 'ripe' to discriminate against Negroes. All right then—the time is always 'ripe' to bring them to justice."

6

Jim Crow Must Go

O N SEPTEMBER 2, 1945, Japan joined Germany and Italy in surrendering to Allied troops, and America's involvement in World War II came to an end. In freeing the survivors of Nazi concentration camps, U.S. soldiers brought to a close the worst campaign of genocide in history. As they wound down from the drama of war, Americans looked inward to find their nation mired in racism. U.S. citizens who decried the persecution of Jews abroad now faced the mistreatment of blacks at home. In World War II, Americans rallied against JEWS ONLY signs on apartments, benches, and eating places in such places as Berlin, but accepted FOR COLORED ONLY markers in Memphis, Birmingham, and Tallahassee.

To no group was this contrast in moral attitudes more apparent than the African-American soldiers who fought in World War II. Like their white compatriots, they defended the United States's ideals of freedom abroad—but they did so under the stigma of segregation. Beginning with training camp, black recruits slept in separate quarters, bought cigarettes and candy in separate stores, and watched movies in blacks-only theaters provided on base. Most recruits, including the young Jackie Robinson, were kept off the sports teams. In battle African-Americans fought in all-black units and often received harsh treatment from their white officers. Many underwent unfair courts-martial (court trials administered by the armed-services legal system for offenses against military law).

Compared with the other segments of the U.S. fighting forces, the army was relatively advanced. The air corps did not admit blacks at all, and the navy only took them on as kitchen help. Though allowed into the air force, African-Americans were not trained to be pilots. It took a lawsuit orchestrated by Thurgood Marshall to give black pilots the right to fly planes in battle.

To change what he viewed as blatant racial prejudice, Marshall took on the case of an experienced flyer who left engineering studies at Howard University to join the air force. Denied the right to be an air force pilot, the young man sued the U.S. government for discrimination. The air force responded by creating an all-black squadron of thirty-three pilots. The victory for Marshall and his client represented a small concession from the air force, whose pilots numbered close to thirty thousand. Still, it was an important symbolic step. Eventually, as the result of pressure exerted by the NAACP and other rights groups, the armed services were integrated. Yet in the Korean War, fought in the early 1950s, black recruits were once again treated unfairly and subjected to an unusually high number of courts-martial. Thanks to Marshall, who flew to the front to help the soldiers, harsh military sentences were reduced for many of them.

When news of the poor treatment of African-American soldiers reached home in the early war years, riots broke out in five major cities. In Harlem, where Marshall lived, angry mobs tore through the streets, smashing store windows and setting fire to cars and debris. These riots vented anger, but accomplished little in the way of reform. Not only did the mistreatment of African-Americans continue through the war, but afterward black soldiers met the same violence and abuse they had endured before going away. In a few instances G.I's heading back home in the South were lynched while still in their uniforms.

Angered by the abuse of veterans and civilians alike, NAACP chief executive Water White led a contingent of reform-minded people to the White House. President Harry S Truman was sympathetic to the plight of blacks, and they hoped he would take steps to outlaw discrimination. White and the others regaled Truman with gruesome stories about the treatment of African-Americans in the South. At the end of the meeting the president exclaimed, "My God, I had no idea that things were as terrible as that. We've got to do something." A short while later Truman set up a commission to study the race problem and strengthen the government's hand in civil rights.

While the Truman commission was busy studying ways to improve race relations, one black veteran of World War II took matters into his own hands. James Stephenson had spent nearly three years in the navy before returning to his hometown of Columbia, Tennessee, after the war. One day in February 1946 the nineteen-year-old veteran accompanied his mother to a repair shop so that she could register a complaint about a poorly fixed radio. Instead of listening to Mrs. Stephenson, however, the white repair man struck her. Enraged by the assault on his mother, Stephenson slugged the white man, sending him crashing through the plate-glass store window. Within minutes the police arrived and carted the mother and son off to jail.

From that point tempers heated quickly. Later that night four white policemen ventured into Columbia's black ghetto. Mistaking the policemen for the first arrivals of a vengeful gang, residents fired guns. No one knew exactly what happened, but several shots struck the officers, who beat a hasty retreat. The violence against Columbia's police did not go unvindicated. At dawn a group of law officials and white townspeople converged on the ghetto and shot everything in sight. In Morton's Funeral Home racists painted the letters *KKK* on a coffin. By early morning local and state police had broken into the homes of African-Americans and herded residents to the streets with their hands over their heads. Of the 106 people arrested, 25 were charged with murder, an offense punishable by death. Immediate trial dates were set.

When word of the Columbia disaster reached Thurgood Marshall in New York, he rushed down to Tennessee. With the help of two local lawyers named Maurice Weaver and Alexander Looby, he took steps to remove the black suspects from contact with white mobs. Most importantly he transferred the trials from Columbia to Lawrenceburg, a backwater town about fifty miles away. To keep himself out of danger, he booked a hotel room in Nashville. From there he had to travel approximately two hundred miles each day to go to and from the trials.

When Marshall and his fellow lawyers first pulled up to the outskirts of Lawrenceburg, they got the message that blacks were not welcome. A sign posted at the city limits read, NIGGER READ AND RUN. DON'T LET THE SUN GO DOWN ON YOU HERE. IF YOU CAN'T READ, RUN ANYWAY. Fortunately the climate inside the courtroom was friendlier. The jury in the Lawrenceburg trials acquitted all but two of the defendants. Later on they acquitted the remaining two. Marshall was elated by the verdict, but realized he still had to wend his way through hostile territory to get back to Nashville. On the way he, Looby, and Weaver would have to pass by Columbia, where news of the verdicts had touched off anger.

The first sign of trouble appeared as Marshall's car crossed the bridge leading out of Columbia. Parked in the middle of the highway was a gray car that Marshall passed by veering off onto the shoulder. Within seconds of his doing so he heard the wailing siren of a police car and pulled over. An officer sauntered up to his car and accused him of carrying illegal whiskey. After searching the car for the nonexistent whiskey, the officer let the attorneys go. But a few miles down the road he stopped them again and accused Marshall of being drunk. Ordering Looby and Weaver back to Nashville, the officer escorted Marshall to his squad car and sped off. Looby and Weaver watched helplessly as Marshall was driven off down a dark road by the Duck River, a favorite lynching spot.

Fortunately for Marshall and the civil rights struggle, Looby and Weaver did not follow orders that night. Instead of heading back to Nashville, they pursued the squad car. With the attorneys' car on their tail, the officers did not stop at the Duck River, but pushed on to Columbia. There they stopped in front of the office of the magistrate (law officer) and ordered Marshall to go inside. Afraid of getting shot in the back for allegedly escaping custody, Marshall refused. The angry police then took him out of the car and shoved him inside the door to appear before the magistrate. Known for his tough stance with drinkers, the magistrate gave Marshall a breath test. "This man isn't drunk," the honest official scoffed, "he hasn't even had a drink." Marshall was set free to once again face the anger of the local police.

Hoping to shake the officers from their trail, Looby and Weaver traded cars with a friend. With Marshall by their side, they slipped unnoticed out of Columbia. The friend wasn't so lucky, however. Receiving the treatment intended for the lawyers, he was followed by police, dragged from his car, and beaten to within an inch of his life. When Marshall heard about the assault, he was outraged. From his hotel room in Nashville he fired off an angry telegram to the U.S. attorney general: "THIS TYPE OF INTIMIDATION OF [LAWYERS] DEFENDING PERSONS CHARGED WITH CRIME CANNOT GO UNNOTICED. . . . WE DEMAND AN IMMEDIATE INVESTIGATION."

The Columbia episode was not the first, nor would it be the last time Marshall risked his welfare to help clients in need. The Fund, Inc., attorney slept in cars if he had to, he ate on the run, and he usually got fewer than four hours' sleep a night. His presence in remote courtrooms lent encouragement to powerless individuals or to threatened civil rights attorneys who otherwise might have given up. As his colleague Roy Wilkins said of him, "All through those years he was there, tall, calm, implacable, briefcase in hand, arguments ready." Occasionally his cases in small towns and villages worked their way up to the Supreme Court. By 1946 he had won three of the four cases he brought before the Court. In tribute to his outstanding record both at the Supreme Court and in the field, the NAACP awarded him the 1946 Spingarn Medal. Named after Joel E. Spingarn, a founding member of the civil rights organization, the medal was distributed each year to an African-American who accomplished "the highest or noblest achievement."

Though he won prestigious awards and often associated with powerful people, Marshall never lost sight of the individuals he called the little Joes. His colleague, attorney Marion Wynn Perry, recalled, "He had this enormous ability to relate. He was not only *of* them—he was *with* them." Marshall's sympathy for the people he encountered grew with each experience, as did his shock at the extreme poverty he saw in the rural South. "One place in Mississippi, we were eating and talking to people," he recalled later, "and a little kid, I guess 12 or 14, a little bright-eyed kid, saw that I was eating an orange. I said, 'Hey, you want one of these?' He said, 'Yeah.' So I gave him one and he just bit into it. He didn't peel it. You know why? It was the first time he had ever seen an orange. That will tell you what we had in those days."

After World War II Marshall and others at the NAACP decided to attack "separate but equal" head on. In a closed meeting with William Hastie and Walter White in 1945, Marshall decided to "go for the whole hog." Instead of arguing for equalized facilities for whites and blacks, he would now argue for an end to segregation.

He got his first chance to argue this line in 1946 with a case challenging segregation on interstate buses. Irene Morgan, an African-American, insisted she had the right to sit near the front of a Greyhound bus headed from Virginia to Maryland. Since the bus was traveling between states where no single state law could apply, Ms. Morgan argued that she didn't have to sit in the area designated for blacks by Virginia law. The bus driver, clearly in disagreement, called in the authorities. Irene Morgan was arrested and fined ten dollars, a sum equivalent to a much greater amount today. Following her arrest, Ms. Morgan sued the state of Virginia. Eventually the case climbed the legal ladder to the Supreme Court, where Thurgood Marshall was eager to use the new strategy worked out by Fund, Inc.

When Marshall argued *Morgan v. Virginia* before the Supreme Court in 1946, he employed arguments that had both practical and moral significance. On the practical level, he said that enforcing segregation laws on interstate buses would place a heavy burden on interstate transportation because the laws in each locality and state were so different. For the moral argument, he relied on the ideals Americans had just fought for in World War II: "Today we are just emerging from a war in which all of the people of the United States were joined in a death struggle against the apostles of racism. How much clearer, therefore, must it be today . . . that the national business of interstate commerce is not to be disfigured by . . . racial notions alien to our national ideals." The justices responded to Marshall's stirring words and ruled segregation illegal on interstate buses. Another major victory was won.

After *Morgan v. Virginia* Marshall turned his attention to restrictive covenants, the private agreements between real estate sellers and buyers that kept blacks out of all-white neighborhoods. In signing a restrictive covenant, a home buyer agreed never to sell or rent to a person of an undesirable race, national origin, or religion. By this means African-Americans, Jews, Asian-Americans, and other minority groups were barred from apartment buildings, neighborhoods, or entire towns. Though many had tried, not one contestant had succeeded in overturning the covenants in the U.S. court system. Time and again African-Americans and other minority groups were told that nothing prevents private individuals from entering into contracts regarding their own property.

In 1947 an African-American family decided to challenge restrictive covenants once again. Orsel McGhee and his wife wanted to live in a white Detroit neighborhood, and they did not want the courts telling them that restrictive covenants could keep them out. Their white next-door neighbors, though, had every intention of doing just that. Soon after they found out that the McGhees had sidestepped the restrictive covenants and bought a house, Mr. and Mrs. Sipes took the case to court. There, the white family succeeded in barring the McGhees from moving in. The McGhees appealed the Michigan court decision to the Supreme Court.

At the Supreme Court the McGhee case was combined with other recent lawsuits concerning restrictive covenants. When the Supreme Court hears several lawsuits dealing with the same issue, it groups the cases under one name, usually that of the first case to be logged in on the official docket, or list. In this instance the combined restrictive-covenant cases were given the new name of *Shelly v. Kramer*. They were argued by an impressive team of lawyers, one of whom was Marshall's old friend Charles Houston. Marshall remained in charge of the McGhee case.

To overturn the legality of restrictive covenants, Marshall took a new approach. Instead of relying solely on legal arguments, he included sociological ones. Marshall pointed out the social damage inflicted on society through discrimination in housing. Restrictive covenants, he said, created an "appalling deterioration of African-American living conditions." They forced blacks to live in overcrowded black neighborhoods that became slums rife with "disease, crime, vice, racial tension, and mob violence." "The case," he went on to say, "is not a matter of enforcing an isolated private agreement. It is a test as to whether we will have a united nation or a nation divided into areas and ghettoes solely on racial and religious lines."

In his plea Marshall was aided by the sympathetic views of President Truman. Eager to strike down restrictive covenants, Truman ordered the U.S. Justice Department to intervene in the *Shelly v. Kramer* cases. Responding to the president's wishes, the U.S. solicitor general submitted an *amicus curiae*, or "friend of the court" brief outlining the government's point of view. It marked the first time in history that the U.S. government got involved in a civil dispute between two individuals. For Truman, shocked by the urban violence that had swept the nation a few years earlier, it was a crucial step to ease racial tension.

The combined efforts of the U.S. government and Marshall's team of legal experts had their intended effect. In May 1948 the Supreme Court ruled restrictive covenants illegal. Though the decision's enforcement would require thousands of additional court cases, its impact was immediate. By 1952, 21,000 African-American families had moved into formerly restricted housing units in Chicago alone. The nation was taking its first tentative steps to reverse years of discrimination.

Fanning the winds of reform was a new humanitarianism that surged as a result of World War II. In the immediate postwar years membership in the NAACP alone peaked at an all-time high of 500,000 members. Hopeful of avoiding another war, growing numbers of Americans pushed for peace and justice at home. Many white veterans who witnessed the bravery of black comrades on the battlefield were ashamed of the treatment they received on U.S. soil. Adding to this pressure for reform was the United States' new "cold war" with the Soviet Union, which had resulted in a contest of propaganda between the two nations. Each wanted to prove that its system of government was better. America's efforts to boost its image to the world were seriously hampered by its obvious mistreatment of blacks. Meanwhile many blacks had secured the means to speak up for themselves. Migration of African-Americans from rural to urban areas had created a sizable black middle class composed of doctors, lawyers, accountants, and other professionals. Well paid and well educated, this reform-minded group began to exercise political clout.

Fortunately President Truman stepped into a leadership role at this critical juncture in the nation's history. In 1947, his voice ringing with emotion, Truman delivered a nationally broadcast speech outlining his proposals for civil rights. In the same year the Truman commission issued *To Secure These Rights*, a report offering forty recommendations to advance fair treatment of African-Americans. Prime among them was a call to end segregation. Significantly the commission flatly stated that "the separate but equal doctrine has failed." Their no-holds-barred report served as a blueprint of reform for the next couple of decades.

Acting on his commission's proposals, Truman took strong measures. He asked Congress to pass laws against lynching, the poll tax, and segregation on interstate buses, among other demands. By executive decree he integrated the armed services. One piece of legislation that had broad impact on African-Americans was the G.I. Bill. Providing government funds to World War II veterans who signed up for school, the bill opened new vistas of educational opportunities for African-American G.I.'s. At the same time it put pressure on predominantly white institutions to admit the flood of qualified black applicants. Few professional schools were open to blacks in the mid-1940s. In the entire South there was only one school each for blacks who wanted to become lawyers, doctors, or pharmacists. Though whites could choose from among thirty-six engineering schools, blacks had none.

Encouraged by Truman's rejection of "separate but equal," the changes wrought by the G.I. Bill, and the wave of reforms, Marshall set out to demolish segregation in schools. He would start with graduate schools, the "soft underbelly" of the educational system. Marshall's next important lawsuit centered around Ada Lois Sipuel, a qualified black applicant turned down by the University of Oklahoma Law

School. When her case reached the Supreme Court, Marshall decided to use the same sociological approach that worked so well in *Shelly v. Kramer*. Citing the research of experts in the field, Marshall and his Fund team noted, "Exclusion of any one group on the basis of race automatically imputes a badge of inferiority to the excluded group—an inferiority that has no basis in fact." They argued that "the role of the lawyer . . . is often that of a lawmaker, a 'social mechanic,' and a 'social inventor.' A profession which produces future legislators and social inventors to whom will fall the social responsibilities of our society, cannot do so on a segregated basis."

The "social mechanics" on the Supreme Court did not agree with Marshall's contention this time. In 1948 they ruled that the University of Oklahoma had abided by the Fourteenth Amendment in setting up a separate, makeshift law school for Ada Sipuel. Though later the university relented and allowed blacks into the law school, their action did not come soon enough to prevent the significant defeat for Marshall at the Supreme Court.

Fortunately Marshall got several more chances to defeat "separate but equal" at the graduate-school level. The first arose when Herman Marion Sweatt, an African-American letter carrier, applied to the University of Texas Law School at Austin but was refused admission under the school's no-blacks policy. When Sweatt sued, the university hurriedly put together a small, unaccredited law school in the basement of a building. Dissatisfied with the inferior facilities, Sweatt eventually petitioned his case through the courts.

When Marshall arrived in Austin to handle *Sweatt*

71

v. Painter (the president of the university), he told a reporter, "I think we've humored the South long enough and it's only by lawsuits and legislation that we'll ever teach reactionaries the meaning of the Fourteenth Amendment." Displaying the bravado of a champion boxer about to enter the ring, Marshall predicted, "This is going to be a real showdown fight against Jim Crow in education." Amazingly the real "showdown" fight against Jim Crow was waged by white students at the university. In an unprecedented show of support for Herman Sweatt, a vocal group of more than two hundred students at the university banded together to organize a local chapter of the NAACP, the first ever on a white Southern campus. These students organized protests, wrote letters on Sweatt's behalf, and solicited funds for his legal defense. Just before the trial two thousand university students staged a demonstration in his support.

Despite the widespread sympathy for Sweatt, his case did not fare well in federal appeals court. During the trial Marshall was up against an attorney renowned for his white-supremacist views. The judge, equally hostile, did nothing to prevent the attorney from making racist remarks during the trial. The remarks infuriated Marshall, who barely controlled his temper. James Nabrit, Jr., a lawyer on the Fund team, recalled the humorous way in which Marshall contained his rage. "He was fuming over the judge in Austin," Nabrit remembered, "and he said to me before court one morning, 'I'm gonna tell that judge what I think of him today.' I told him to take it easy. He said nothing in court, but after the case was over and we were all heading for the cars, there was Thurgood standing over in the corner apparently muttering to himself. When he came back to join us, I asked him what that was all about, and he said, 'I told you I was gonna tell that judge what I thought of him—and I just did.' "

Fund, Inc., lost the case. The Texas court ruled that the basement law school set up for Sweatt satisfied requirements for "separate but equal" facilities. Not content with this outcome, Marshall appealed the decision to the Supreme Court, and Sweatt went back to his job at the post office. It took over a year for the Court to agree to hear Sweatt's case. During that time Marshall turned his attention to another antisegregation case at the University of Oklahoma.

The Oklahoma lawsuit centered around the predicament of George W. McLaurin, a sixty-eight-year-old college professor admitted to the university to earn his Ph.D. in Education. McLaurin suffered almost inhuman conditions at the school, where he was completely segregated from white students. Not allowed to sit in the classrooms, McLaurin was given a desk just outside the doors. From his seat the distinguished professor strained his ears to listen to the lectures. During meals he ate alone at a designated table in the cafeteria during times when no white students were present. The same strict segregation applied in the library, where McLaurin sat in the balcony at a screened-off table far from other students.

When university officials heard that Marshall planned to take the case to the Supreme Court, they got nervous. To ward off bad publicity and increase their chances of winning the case, officials made some hasty and ridiculous improvements in McLaurin's status at the school. They allowed him in the classrooms, but required him to sit at a desk surrounded by a railing labeled RESERVED FOR COLORED. In addition they moved his lone library table from the balcony to the main floor. At the cafeteria they told McLaurin that white students could be present in the room while he ate by himself at his table. Surveying these changes, Marshall and McLaurin concluded that they did little to alter the humiliating conditions.

In April 1950 Marshall got his big chance to argue both *Sweatt v. Painter* and *McLaurin v. Oklahoma State Regents*, two cases the Supreme Court grouped together. In his arguments for both Marshall added a new element to the legal and sociological lines of approach. In the case of *Sweatt* he asked the Justices, "What makes a great law school?" He then answered the question by pointing to the "intangible" factors that could not be measured in physical terms—the school's reputation and the achievements of its alumni, for example. He went on to argue that the unaccredited three-room law school provided to Sweatt could not possibly measure up to the University of Texas Law School. Even if the facilities had been equalized, the intangible factors would still make the newer school inferior.

Turning to McLaurin's case, Marshall punctuated his arguments with a dramatic description of the professor's status at the school. "He must sit by himself outside the door of the classroom," he informed the justices. "He studies at a *separate desk* in the library, hidden by half a carload of newspapers. His dining room is a small space known as 'The Jug,' and he eats *conversationless* and *alone*. The only purpose of this *inhuman* treatment is to demonstrate that McLaurin is an inferior being and altogether unfit to associate with the white race."

As in earlier cases Marshall called for an end to "separate but equal," hoping to overturn the famous *Plessy v. Ferguson* decision of 1896. Though the Court came near to doing so, it did not overturn *Plessy* in its decision. It did, however, hand Marshall a stunning triumph by ruling unanimously in favor of both Sweatt and McLaurin. In his opinion, Chief Justice Vinson relied on the Fourteenth Amendment to strike down the unequal treatment of the two African-American students. But he also took into consideration Marshall's arguments about the "intangible" factors that make schools unequal. In doing so, he established a crucial precedent for future education cases. To overturn *Plessy*, though, Marshall would have to wait for another opportunity.

Just after delivering arguments for *Sweatt* and *McLaurin*, Marshall received disheartening news: On April 22 "social engineer" Charles Houston died of heart failure at the age of fifty-four. Marshall agreed to serve as a pallbearer at his funeral. Charles Houston had trained nearly every young lawyer at the NAACP. Declaring "I would rather die on my feet than live on my knees," the tireless advocate devoted his life to the cause of civil rights. With Houston's passing, Marshall lost the friend and mentor who had incited his passion for the law and cheered him on through struggles he never thought he would win.

Just before he died, Charles Houston filed a lawsuit in Washington, D.C., on behalf of black students trying to attend the all-white Sousa Junior High School. A few weeks later, in May, Marshall and his team of lawyers filed a federal lawsuit in Charleston, South Carolina, on behalf of grade-school children asking for equal education. The two cases represented the beginnings of *Brown v. Board of Education*. For the next four years Marshall would collaborate with Houston—at least in spirit—by carrying the banner of equal rights in one of the greatest legal campaigns ever known.

7

Brown v. Board of Education

CLARENDON COUNTY, South Carolina, was a place where the words *separate* and *equal* could hardly be uttered in the same breath. Most blacks in the county lived in poor neighborhoods, worked at low-paying jobs, and attended inferior schools. Segregation was so strictly enforced in Clarendon that separate days were set up for blacks and whites at the annual county fair.

Though segregation reached into every area of life, it had its most noticeable effect in the schools. Black children in Clarendon attended separate, and miserably unequal, institutions of learning. Every year the state of South Carolina spent four times as much on the education of each white child than it spent for each black. There were approximately 275 white children who went to well-appointed schools equipped with playgrounds, sports fields, libraries, and other facilities. The 800 black students, however, were crammed into three dilapidated wooden buildings with no plumbing or central heating. In the town of Summerton, where the black children's school did not have enough chairs and desks, many just sat on the floor.

One teacher had to contend with 104 pupils at one time. The students shivered with cold in the winter and had to use outhouses in the backyard for toilets.

To get to and from school, the African-American children walked while their white fellow students rode buses. For some the walk was a long one, as much as six miles. One student, Plummie Parsons, left her home every morning at five-thirty so that she could make it to school on time. Along the way the white children's bus would pass her. She recalled that the experience was a humiliating one. "On rainy mornings they'd splash us if we didn't back out of the way," she remembered. "On cold winter mornings, when many of us were freezing, they'd go by with us knowing that the white children were comfortable and warm in the buses. But then in the nice weather, when the bus windows were open, the white children would often taunt us as they passed, or even throw things at us."

At first Harry Briggs, a black U.S. Navy veteran and father of five, didn't believe there was anything the black parents could do about the situation. "We didn't know any different. The colored had their place, and the whites had theirs. And that's how we supposed things were just naturally." In 1949, however, Briggs changed his mind. Along with about 120 black residents of Summerton, he signed a petition addressed to R. W. Elliott and other members of Clarendon County's all-white school board. The petitioners politely requested buses and better schools for the county's black children. Helping the parents in their efforts was the local pastor, Rev. Joseph De Laine.

No sooner had the black parents delivered their petition than the whites began retaliation. Harry Briggs immediately got fired from his job as a gas-station attendant. Mr. De Laine watched his house burn to the ground while firefighters looked on. Most other petitioners were harassed into withdrawing their names. Even whites sympathetic to the petitioners' cause were bullied into submission by their extremist neighbors. The campaign of intimidation worked: Within a few months only twenty-two names remained on the petition.

Instead of giving in to the pressure, however, the Reverend Mr. De Laine contacted the NAACP. A few months later Thurgood Marshall and Spotswood Robinson of Fund, Inc., filed *Briggs v. Elliott* in the federal district court at Charleston. In their legal papers, Marshall and Robinson requested an order for equalization of schools in Clarendon County. In a more surprising move they asked the court to declare South Carolina's segregation unconstitutional.

News of the case reached every corner of South Carolina. On May 28, 1951, the day of the hearings, a large crowd assembled at the courthouse. Only a small portion of them could be seated inside. The others remained outdoors, listening for reports of the trial through open windows. Seated among the visitors in the courtroom that day was Bennie Parsons, one of the original signers of the petition. "We were warned by white folks not to go down [to Charleston]," he recalled. "They said don't go because there will be 'blood in the streets.' We went anyway, and there was no blood."

Briggs v. Elliott had Clarendon County school officials worried. Threatened with an end to segregation, they decided to steer the court away from considering the major issue of whether segregation itself was unconstitutional. Instead they openly admitted that the black schools were inferior and they promised to upgrade them. If upgraded, the black schools would be "separate but equal." *Briggs v. Elliott* would then become a moot case because the conditions for bringing the lawsuit no longer applied. Upgrading schools was a small price to pay for maintaining segregation.

Countering their argument, Marshall was out to prove that separate schools could never be equal. He had gathered information from expert witnesses in sociology, psychology, and other fields that demonstrated the negative effect of segregation on black children. Interpreting their findings, Marshall came to the conclusion that segregation gave those children psychological and social problems that no amount of equalizing would overcome. During the dramatic courtroom proceedings Marshall called nine expert witnesses to the stand to explain this idea. One by one they presented strong and moving evidence of the fact that black children's self-esteem and chances for success were decimated by being forced into all-black schools.

The best-known among the witnesses, Dr. Kenneth Clark, was a social psychologist who had conducted experiments in Summerton's school. In the experiment he held out a white doll and a black doll to each of sixteen black children, ages six to nine. He then asked the children which doll they liked the best. Ten of them, he said, chose the white doll, and eleven said the black doll looked "bad." Explaining the results of an experiment he conducted at a different school, Dr. Clark told the court that one little African-American girl who preferred the white doll described the black doll as "ugly" and "dirty." She dissolved into tears when she was asked which doll was most like her. From these experiments Dr. Clark concluded that "segregation was, is, the way in which a society tells a group of human beings that they are inferior to other groups of human beings in the society."

Agreeing with Dr. Clark was another expert witness, psychologist Dr. David Krech. He told the court that a black child enrolled in a segregated school system "will probably never recover from whatever harmful effect racial prejudice and discrimination can wreak." Krech was followed by Dr. Robert Redfield, an anthropologist who testified to the fact that there is no scientific basis for the separation of white and black children. The intelligence and aptitude of the two races are equal.

Extraordinary as it was, the testimony provided by Marshall's witnesses failed to persuade the three-judge panel that segregation should be ruled unconstitutional. In a decision handed down on June 23, 1951, the judges ordered Clarendon County to equalize schools for black and white schoolchildren. The judges refused, however, to grant Marshall's second and more sweeping demand to end segregation in South Carolina. William Kunstler, a well-known civil rights attorney who attended the trial, believes that this was because Marshall's demands were contradictory. Marshall, according to Kunstler, wanted "to have his cake and eat it too." He argued for equalization under the "separate but equal" doctrine and at the same time asserted that "separate but equal" was unconstitutional.

The judge most bothered by the contradiction was J. Waties Waring, the same man who, presiding over a trial years earlier, had told South Carolina it was

81

time to rejoin the Union and let blacks vote. An opponent of segregation himself, Waring pressed Marshall during the trial to make up his mind. When the decision of his fellow judges was announced, Waring delivered a vigorous dissenting opinion. Calling segregation evil, he said that "the system of segregation in education adopted and practiced in the state of South Carolina must go and go now. Segregation is [by definition] inequality."

Marshall couldn't have wished for a stronger statement from a federal judge. He planned to use it when he appealed the decision before the Supreme Court. With that goal firmly in mind, Marshall cleared his papers from the attorneys' table the last day of hearings. On his way out he got a taste of local racist sentiment. "If you show your black ass in Clarendon County ever again," a white attorney snarled, "you're a dead man." As he did with most threats, Marshall ignored this one. It served as a timely reminder that the hate-provoking practice of segregation had to end. Judge J. Waties Waring had received a different sort of reminder. Late one evening angry whites placed a burning cross in front of his window. Eventually similar pressure forced him to move out of South Carolina.

Many people on both sides of the segregation argument viewed *Briggs v. Elliott* as a defeat for Marshall. Among his vociferous critics in the African-American community were those who said that he had set back the civil rights struggle by moving too fast to press for change. Marshall strongly disagreed. Far from sputtering out in defeat, *Briggs v. Elliott* was shooting for the Supreme Court, right where he wanted it. Like a general who divides his troops into several fronts in order to launch an important attack, Marshall lined up segregation cases from five areas of the country. In the years 1950 to 1952 he joined Fund lawyers in bringing the cases to the lower courts and ushering them through the legal system all the way to the top. Once the five cases were scheduled for hearings at the Supreme Court, Marshall's team trained its legal ammunition on Washington, D.C., where the final assault on school segregation was about to begin.

The first of the five cases to be placed on the Supreme Court docket was *Brown v. Board of Education of Topeka, Kansas*. Filed on behalf of the Reverend Mr. Oliver Brown and twelve black parents and their children, the lawsuit challenged Kansas's segregation laws. As in the *Briggs* case in South Carolina, a three-judge panel in federal court failed to rule Kansas's segregation unconstitutional. Fund lawyer Robert Carter then petitioned the Supreme Court.

In the fall of 1952, when the Supreme Court agreed to hear both *Brown* and *Briggs*, the justices added three more Fund cases to the docket: *Bolling v. Sharpe*, the case begun by Charles Houston, challenged segregated schools in Washington, D.C.; *Davis v. County School Board of Prince Edward County* targeted separate schools in Virginia; and *Gebhard v. Belton* pinpointed those in Delaware. To make record keeping simple, the five cases were consolidated under the name *Brown v. Board of Education*, but they were each argued separately. Marshall took charge of *Briggs v. Elliott* and directed the Fund team on overall strategy.

To prepare for oral arguments at the Supreme Court scheduled for December 9, Marshall worked feverishly. Ten days before the Court date, he set up a combination office-residence in Washington's Statler Hotel. For twenty-three hours a day he picked the brains of the best lawyers he knew. Eating little and smoking too many cigarettes, he rehearsed the arguments intended to topple Jim Crow. The future of millions of youths were at stake. Fund lawyers had filed the cases as class-action suits, which meant that the decision in these cases would apply to every African-American schoolchild who attended segregated schools. *Brown v. Board of Education* had the potential to affect the lives of approximately 2.5 million black children spread across seventeen states and the District of Columbia.

On the morning of December 9 an amazing sight greeted Marshall as he stepped out of the car that pulled up in front of the Supreme Court building. Hundreds of people lined the steps that led to the massive bronze doors. Blacks and whites stood side by side, hoping to gain entrance to the momentous trial about to begin. Over the colonnade portico that led to the bronze doors, a large inscription was chiseled into the marble. It read, EQUAL JUSTICE UNDER LAW. The civil rights attorney who had spent his entire adult life arguing for that principle hoped that today he could convince the nation that it applied to African-American schoolchildren.

Inside, the courtroom was packed, and five hundred people spilled out into the halls. Marshall had never seen so many spectators in the building. He knew the Supreme Court well by now. As director of Fund, Inc., he had argued fifteen cases on its premises and had lost only two. Today, full of important people and expectant faces, the courtroom seemed even more imposing than usual. It was a formal chamber, built with

Italian marble and outfitted with polished mahogany furnishings. Surrounding the room were marble columns at the top of which large panels illustrated the virtues and vices of man—Justice, Truth, Corruption, Malice, and others.

With little time to appreciate the sumptuous decor, Marshall made his way to the attorneys' table and mentally rehearsed the procedure of the day. He knew that a total of ten hours were scheduled for oral arguments in the five cases. Each case was allotted two hours, and *Briggs* came second on the docket. Marshall would have exactly one hour to argue his side of *Briggs* before giving the floor to the opposing attorney. As he neared the end of his argument, Marshall would have to watch for two lights to appear on the lectern in front of him. A white light would tell him he had five minutes left. A flashing red light signaled that his time was up. His challenge was to finish his presentation before the red light flashed. The Supreme Court justices were sticklers for time and tolerated no deviation from the schedule. They were known to cut off attorneys in mid-sentence. If Marshall went over the time limit by as much as a few seconds, he would be asked to stop talking and lose much of the force of his argument.

Marshall looked up to eye his opponent, the elegant, white-haired John W. Davis. In asking Davis to represent them in their case, the Clarendon County school board had selected one of the great constitutional law experts in the country. Davis had argued 140 cases before the Supreme Court and he intended to crown his career with a victory in this one. A former congressman and presidential candidate, Davis had also served as solicitor general (the U.S. government's top trial lawyer) and ambassador to Great Britain. He had even turned down a position as a justice of the Supreme Court. Davis's eloquence was legendary.

As a student Marshall had often taken time off to listen to the great lawyer argue at the Supreme Court. Now he would have to confront him as a formidable opponent. Marshall was already well acquainted with his views. A Southerner, Davis believed that desegregation was a matter to be decided at the local level, by the people whose lives would most be affected. To him federal-imposed segregation was drastic and premature.

Toward noon the crowd grew silent when the official of the Court rapped his gavel to announce, "The Honorable, the Chief Justice and Associate Justices of the Supreme Court of the United States!" Everyone stood as Chief Justice Fred Vinson and the eight associate justices, wearing the customary black robes, took their seats behind the mahogany bench. The Court official rapped the gavel once again and the proceedings began. *Brown v. Board of Education* was under way.

Marshall watched nervously as his colleague, Robert L. Carter, approached the lectern to argue *Brown*, the first case on the docket. Within a few minutes Carter set forth Fund's proposal to overturn the historic *Plessy* decision. He had hardly uttered the words before he was interrupted by the abrasive voice of Justice Felix Frankfurter. "Are you saying," Frankfurter asked, "that . . . 'separate but equal' is *not* a doctrine that is relevant at the primary school level?" The associate justice was bothered by the suggestion that the Supreme Court could have been wrong all the years since 1896, when *Plessy* was affirmed. Marshall winced. He realized that convincing the justices to overturn the *Plessy* "separate but equal" doctrine was going to be a lot harder than he thought.

The high point of the proceedings arrived when Marshall got up to argue the next case, *Briggs v. Elliott*. Without hesitating, Marshall dove into the heart of his argument, an attack on *Plessy*. "The trouble with the doctrine of 'separate but equal,' " he told the justices, "is that it assumes that two things are equal." Marshall then explained why separate institutions for blacks and whites could never be equal. He pointed to the findings of Dr. Clark and the other expert witnesses. He told the Court that segregation impaired black children's motivation and self-image, conferring a "badge of inferiority" that lasted a lifetime.

Speaking next, John W. Davis mustered all the dramatic and rhetorical flair he had cultivated in his long career. Quoting the words of W.E.B. Du Bois, he argued that upheaving the age-old tradition of segregation in the South would upset blacks and whites alike, causing misunderstandings and violence. Moving on to constitutional issues, he asserted that Congress never intended to strike down school segregation when it passed the Fourteenth Amendment in 1868. If they had, he said, they would not have allowed segregation to continue right in Washington, D.C., which is legally under Congress's jurisdiction.

Interrupting Davis's arguments, Justice Harold Burton threw him a legal challenge. "If the Constitution is a living document," the associate justice contended, "it must be interpreted in light of the conditions of the times." Scoffing at this "living document" theory, which was also championed by Marshall and others, Davis argued for a narrow interpretation of the historic document. He wanted to rely on what was written in the Constitution, not what was intended. He also thought the Court should uphold its previous decisions in coming up with an opinion in *Brown*. Referring to the Court's long history of legalizing segregation, he concluded, "There is no reason to reverse the findings of ninety years."

Oral arguments for the five cases in *Brown v. Board of Education* took three grueling days. By the time they ended at 3:50 P.M. on December 11, the two sides had fought to a standstill, and neither Marshall nor Davis had emerged the victor. The Court was still not ready to make its decision. In order to weigh the constitutional issues at stake, the justices needed more information from the attorneys. Was the Fourteenth Amendment intended to ban segregation? Does the Supreme Court have the jurisdiction to stop segregation—or is it the job of Congress? If the Court were to rule in favor of desegregation, how could it put the decision into effect throughout school districts in the nation?

The attorneys would soon receive these questions in memo from the Court. In the meantime they were unsure about whether the justices were ready to form an opinion. John W. Davis guessed they were. He left the courtroom that day a confident man. On his way out the door he whispered to a colleague, "I think we've got it won." His buoyancy contrasted sharply with Marshall's mood. The tired attorney walked out of the Supreme Court without a trace of hope. Assessing his performance earlier that day at lunch, he had told those present, "The truth is, fellas, I wasn't very good." Like most spectators in the courtroom, he had marveled at Davis's dramatic delivery and his grasp of constitutional law. "He makes it sound like pages of history," Marshall admitted.

Fortunately Marshall got one more chance to flaunt his own considerable powers of persuasion. In June 1953 he received a notice from the Supreme Court scheduling rearguments of the case for the fall. Included in the memo were the questions the justices wanted answered. Determined to beat the opposition this time, Marshall organized fact-finding conferences of experts in the fields of U.S. history and constitutional law. Attorneys from all over the nation converged on the New York offices of Fund, Inc., to offer their advice. With their help, the Fund team spent months preparing a brief. But when they showed it to Marshall, he shook his head in disapproval. It wasn't strong enough. The intent of the Fourteenth Amendment had not been addressed properly. It would never pass muster with the justices. "I gotta argue these cases," Marshall complained, "and if I try this approach, those fellows will shoot me down in flames." Finally he settled on an approach he liked. The brief was filed with the Court, and Marshall then waited nervously for the day he would have to argue it.

When, on December 8, 1953, Marshall stepped up to the lectern to argue his portion of *Brown v. Board*, he faced a radically changed Court. Chief Justice Vinson had just died, and his place was filled by a new Chief Justice named Earl Warren. A savvy politician, Warren had served as California's governor. He was sympathetic to desegregation efforts and understood the tremendous significance of the case before him. As *Brown* progressed, Warren did his best to orchestrate a unanimous decision among the justices. Fortunately his task was made somewhat easier by the antisegregation sentiments expressed by the official representative of the U.S. Department of Justice during the trial. The assistant attorney general testified in front of the Court that the government's position was that segregation could not be upheld under the Fourteenth Amendment.

The new chief justice was impressed by Marshall, whose arguments in this second round were clear, forceful, and convincing. He recalled that Marshall delivered them "cold as steel," in contrast to Davis, who displayed so much emotion that he broke down on several occasions. Marshall grappled head on with the set of questions posed by the justices the previous spring. Concerning the jurisdiction issue, he told the justices they had every right to rule on segregation. Congress had shirked its responsibility in this area. Responding to the more difficult constitutional question, he insisted that there was no doubt that the framers of the Fourteenth Amendment sought to give blacks the same rights as those enjoyed by whites— not *separate* rights, but equal rights. "What's important," he stated flatly, "is that we get the principle established—segregation is not legal."

The man who had spent a good part of his life traveling through the South then added his plainspoken wisdom. Referring to the fact that black and white children often play quite happily together, he said, "I got the feeling on hearing the discussion yesterday that [you think] when you put a white child in school with a whole lot of colored children, the child would fall apart or something. Everybody knows that is not true. These same kids in Virginia and South Carolina—and I have seen them do it—they play in the streets together, they play on their farms together, they go down the road together, they *separate* to go to school. . . . They have to be separated *in school.*''

After Marshall finished his talk, Davis took the floor to deliver his final plea to the Court. He described how the *Plessy* doctrine and the practice of segregation had become embedded, not only in America's law but also in its way of life. He warned the Court that terrible consequences would result from a sudden change in that way of life. The Court could order such a change, he said, but ''Dear God, at what a cost! We would do better to put Negro children in schools where they are *wanted.*''

After the courtroom emptied on the last day of hearings, December 9, 1953, Marshall had to wait five long months for the fateful decision. It came, finally, on May 17, 1954. When the justices walked into the buzzing courtroom that day, Chief Justice Warren noted ''a tenseness that I have not seen equaled before or since.'' The moment's drama gripped everyone, from the chief justice to reporters poised to file dispatches to every corner of the globe. Even Justice Robert Jackson, who had been hospitalized for a heart attack, got dressed and came to Court to participate in the event. As Warren began to read the opinion, the Court fell into rapt attention.

''In approaching the problem,'' Warren ventured, ''we cannot turn the clock back to 1868 when the [Fourteenth] Amendment was adopted, or even to 1896 when *Plessy v. Ferguson* was written. We must consider public education in the light of its full development and its present place in American life throughout the nation.'' Marshall's heart worked overtime as he realized that Warren was sidestepping

91

the thorny question of the framers' intent for the Fourteenth Amendment. Leaning heavily on Marshall's sociological arguments, Warren continued, "Does segregation of children in public schools solely on the basis of race . . . deprive the children of the minority group of equal educational opportunities?" Warren paused here to give his next words their full effect. "We believe that it does. To separate [black children] from others . . . solely because of their race generates a feeling of inferiority . . . that may affect their hearts and minds in a way unlikely ever to be undone." Warren then summed up with the Court's ground-breaking decision: "We conclude, unanimously, that in the field of public education the doctrine of 'separate but equal' has no place."

Stunned by the words, Marshall grabbed his hat and bolted from the courtroom. Finding the nearest telephone, he called Buster at home and Jack Greenberg at the Fund office in New York. As he did so, news bulletins flashed the surprise decision onto television screens and newspapers around the country. When Marshall went back to the NAACP offices, he was greeted with cheers. Roy Wilkins remembered that "Thurgood walked in with a grin as wide as Fifth Avenue. He walked right over and kissed me." Marshall remembered, "I was so happy I was numb." After the initial celebration quieted down, Marshall and the others sat in silence, struck with awe at the immense importance of the decision. Back at the Supreme Court, Justice Felix Frankfurter penned a few words to the chief justice that expressed the pride shared by millions of Americans on May 17, 1954: "This is a day that will live in glory."

UPI/ BETTMANN ARCHIVES

A triumphant Thurgood Marshall with attorneys George E. C. Hayes and James Nabrit, Jr. outside the Supreme Court after Brown v. Board of Education, 1954

8

The Aftermath of *Brown*

S A MILESTONE in civil rights, *Brown v. Board of Education* "lived in glory," but the same could not be said of events in the months and years that followed. When the curtain fell on Jim Crow, he did not exit gracefully. Instead he revived his career with a vengeance, helped by conservative Southerners determined to keep African-Americans "in their place." Many Southerners applauded the *Brown* decision, but in the resulting controversy, extremists won the day. As a consequence, violence and bloodshed inundated the South, much as it had after the Civil War.

John W. Davis had foreseen the violence. When told of the decision in *Brown*, he warned, "There are troubled times ahead." Others who met defeat in *Brown* did not show the same gentlemanly restraint. Southern segregationists were quick to label May 17 Black Monday. Five weeks after the decision Virginia's governor vowed to "use every legal means at my command to continue segregated schools in Virginia." At the Capitol in Washington, 101 congressmen put together a "Southern Manifesto," pledging to do everything legally possible to overturn the Court's decision and prevent its implementation.

Angry words were not the only reaction to come out of the South. On the night of May 17, 1954, the Ku Klux Klan lit fiery crosses of hatred across the South. In Mississippi extremists went on a rampage against the homes and churches of African-Americans. Lynchings continued unabated. Residents of Clarendon County, South Carolina, vented their rage against the Reverend Mr. De Laine by hounding him out of the state. Under threat of death he moved his family to New York City, where he remained for the rest of his life. Harry Briggs, the man whose name appeared in the famous *Briggs v. Elliott* lawsuit, met the same fate. Denied jobs in every state in the South, he finally moved to the Bronx, New York, and lived there until he died. In fact every Clarendon County petitioner was forced to leave South Carolina.

While the *Brown* controversy raged, Marshall faced a devastating problem at home. Immediately after the Supreme Court decision, he discovered that Buster Marshall had lung cancer. The news brought the couple close together for one last period in their lives. When Buster grew too weak to move from bed, Marshall stayed by her side. He shopped for food, cooked her meals, and took care of her as best he could. "She would have done the same for me," he commented sadly. In February 1955 his best friend and wife of over twenty-five years died. "I thought the end of the world had come," he remembered.

Childless, and alone for nearly a year, Marshall ventured a few dates with Cecilia Suyat, a legal secretary who worked at the NAACP, in the fall of 1955. They fell in love and married in December. Marshall used their honeymoon in the Virgin Islands to take a much-needed rest. His new wife, nicknamed Cissy, was a Hawaiian of Filipino descent. Warm and outgoing, she was popular among co-workers. Her even temper exerted a calming influence on the dynamic Marshall. Within a few years the couple gave birth to two children, Thurgood, Jr., born in 1956, and John William, who came along two years later.

Cissy Marshall's support at home gave Marshall strength to confront the enormous task of desegregation ahead of him. Spurred on by the *Brown* decision, the optimistic lawyer estimated that there would be no segregated schools in the United States by the year 1963, the 100th anniversary of the Emancipation Proclamation. Later he realized how wrong that prediction was.

Aside from Southern hostility, Marshall and his staff had to contend with a go-slow loophole left in the Supreme Court's implementation plan. In May 1955 the Supreme Court had come up with a strategy to put *Brown v. Board* into effect. It ordered school districts to desegregate "with all deliberate speed" and gave federal courts powers to enforce the ruling. Marshall did not like the phrase "all deliberate speed," and had argued instead for a set timetable.

"All deliberate speed" meant different things to different people. For several city school systems it meant "right away." Baltimore, Louisville, Saint Louis, to name a few, desegregated their schools within twelve months. By contrast several small school districts in West Virginia took as long as twelve years. Many others avoided the issue altogether until taken to court by Fund, Inc.

In 1956 the Virginia legislature passed massive-resistance laws to get around the *Brown* ruling. Rather than allow a few black children to attend a white school, the governor of Virginia ordered an entire school system closed. For almost five months thirteen thousand schoolchildren of both races were kept out of the classroom. Asked what he planned to do about the stalling in Virginia and elsewhere, Marshall responded, "Virginia we're going to bust wide open! . . . those white crackers are going to get tired of having Negro lawyers beating them every day in court." Likewise, when the pugnacious attorney got word that the state of Georgia planned to fight the *Brown* decision in all of its 159 counties, he said he was going to take all 159 counties to court.

Marshall did not have long to wait to put his threats into action. In the first five years after *Brown* he and his staff filed hundreds of desegregation lawsuits on behalf of schoolchildren and university students. He brought seven major cases to the Supreme Court. One of these was a lawsuit filed on behalf of Arthurine Lucy, a black sharecropper's daughter who wanted to study library science at the University of Alabama. Lucy had been admitted to the university back in 1952. But when she showed up for her first day of classes, school officials told her they had made a mistake because the university did not admit blacks. After Marshall won a decision in her favor at the Supreme Court, she thought she was ready once again to enter the doors of the university.

On February 6, 1956, Marshall escorted Arthurine Lucy to classes. But when they arrived, a mob of more than a thousand agitators tried to pelt her with rocks and eggs. As she ran to hide in a classroom, the crowd outside yelled, "Kill her, kill her." After this incident the university suspended her, supposedly for the safety of all concerned. Marshall then filed a complaint in federal court and got her readmitted. The court's decision lasted only a few hours. Determined to keep her out of the university, officials expelled her for remarks she made about the university during the federal trial.

At this point Marshall and his fellow attorney, Constance Baker Motley, flew to Tuscaloosa, Alabama, to bring the dejected student back to New York. There the NAACP had sponsored a press conference for her. Looking squarely into TV cameras, Lucy vowed, "I shall maintain my faith in my country." Though she managed to maintain her faith in the country, she did not go back to the university right away. It took her several years to screw up the courage to return. It wasn't until nearly a decade after the trouble began that she received her diploma.

A year and a half after this storm a full-blown racial hurricane hit the city of Little Rock, Arkansas. Over the objections of Governor Orval Faubus, the city's school board had enrolled nine black teenagers at all-white Central High School. To squelch the desegregation plan, Governor Faubus ordered Arkansas's national guard to stand by the school doors and prevent the black students from entering. As the beginning of the school year approached, tension mounted to a breaking point.

On the morning of September 4 fifteen-year-old Elizabeth Eckford prepared for her first day of classes at Central High. She put on a freshly ironed dress, donned her sunglasses, and grabbed a notebook on her way out the door to head downtown to school. Unlike most girls getting ready to go to Central High that morning, Elizabeth was black. She was one of the nine African-American students chosen to break the color barrier in Little Rock's school system. She did not know it at the time, but the process of integration would drag her through the worst experiences of her life.

The first sign of trouble appeared as soon as Elizabeth approached the school. Standing in front of it were 250 guardsmen decked out in combat uniforms with their guns ready. Near them a mob of jeering whites yelled out threats and racial slurs to the girl. Realizing that the guardsmen would do nothing to help her, Elizabeth ran to a nearby bus stop. The mob followed, several of whom shrieked that the black student should be brought to the nearest tree and hanged. At last, with the aid of a white sympathizer, Elizabeth escaped and went home. When the other eight black students arrived at the school, they were met by the same angry crowd. For the next three weeks the youths were prevented from walking through the doors of the school.

When Marshall got word of the black students' reception at the school, he was enraged. The first thing he did was obtain a court order forbidding Governor Faubus to interfere with the desegregation plan. Unwilling to take orders from a federal court, the governor ignored it. Worse, on September 23 he removed the national guard and allowed the white mob to wreak havoc at the school. By mid-morning the frenzied crowd had assaulted at least two black reporters covering the scene. They smashed school windows and doors and came close to seizing the terrified nine

MARTIN LUTHER KING MEMORIAL LIBRARY. WASHINGTON. D.C./WASHINGTON STAR COLLECTION

This scene typified extremist backlash against the desegregation ruling in Brown.

students trying to attend classes inside. Only through a police evacuation effort did the Little Rock Nine escape.

At that point in the showdown between state and federal government, President Dwight D. Eisenhower took action. Unlike his forceful predecessor Harry S Truman, Eisenhower was a conservative when it came to civil rights. Yet, faced with the governor's flouting of federal authority—the worst challenge since Civil War days—Eisenhower had no choice but to interfere. On September 25 he sent one thousand federal paratroopers to Central High. In addition he assigned each of the students a bodyguard. Placing the Arkansas national guard under his command, the president ordered them to keep the peace at Central High for the rest of the school year. Eisenhower's action represented the first time the government had used federal troops to discipline a state since 1865. As a result of his efforts, on September 25, Elizabeth Eckford and the other black students marched through a crowd of hostile whites waving confederate flags and entered their new school.

Despite these precautions, violence against the nine students continued throughout the school year. To ward off serious trouble in the future, the school board, in June 1958, asked the federal court to postpone Little Rock's desegregation plans for two and a half years. This maneuver angered Marshall. He knew that a postponement would send the wrong signal to thousands of school districts around the country looking to Little Rock for an example. Hoping for a strong directive from the justices, he took the matter to the Supreme Court. "This case," he told the Court, "involves . . . the very survival of the Rule of Law. The case affords this Court the opportunity to restate . . . all constitutional rights over bigots—big and small."

Eventually the Supreme Court came through for Marshall in two important decisions. Though Governor Faubus scuttled desegregation plans once again by shutting down Central High for the 1958–59 year, he finally gave in. In September 1959 the Little Rock Nine went back to school. Despite continued racial unrest, most of them got their high school diplomas and went on to college. By persevering, the brave teenagers paved the way for the integration of thousands of students in Little Rock and other embattled towns throughout the South. Thanks to their efforts, Central High eventually became a place where blacks and whites mixed with ease. By 1980 African-Americans made up half the school's population and a third of its teachers.

Encouraged by the Supreme Court's strong stance in *Brown*, Marshall had pushed for desegregation in areas beyond education. In 1955 he seized upon the long-awaited opportunity to attack discriminatory laws in Baltimore. African-Americans in that city were still barred from whites-only beaches and bathhouses, just as they had been when Marshall was a boy. Taking up the cause of several black residents who decided to sue, Marshall ushered their case, *Dawson v. Mayor and the City Council of Baltimore*, into the Supreme Court. When the Court struck down Baltimore's statutes as unconstitutional, Marshall felt the same sense of vindication he experienced after getting Donald Murray into the University of Maryland.

Marshall followed the Baltimore lawsuit with others in the areas of professional sports, housing, transportation, and public facilities. Yet despite his hard work and many triumphs, school desegregation plodded along slowly. By the late 1950s only a tiny fraction of African-American students had been placed in integrated schools. Impatient with the sluggish pace, a new generation of civil rights activists pushed for immediate change. Inspired by nonviolent-disobedience tactics of Mahatma Gandhi, Henry David Thoreau, and other historic figures, they used sit-ins, demonstrations, and plain disobedience to achieve their ends. They applied these methods to integrate lunch counters, buses, voting polls, and other important areas in which discrimination was practiced. The progress achieved through *Brown v. Board of Education* disappointed many people. But in informing blacks of their rights and heightening their expectations for change, *Brown* unleashed forces that sustained the great civil rights movement of the 1960s.

One man given hope by *Brown* was a young Baptist minister in Montgomery, Alabama, named Martin Luther King, Jr. In 1954 he volunteered his services to the local NAACP. Two years later he helped found the Southern Christian Leadership Conference (SCLC) and launched a campaign for civil rights that changed history. King's first project was sparked by Rosa Parks, a black seamstress and NAACP volunteer who refused to give up her bus seat to a white woman as required by Montgomery law.

Parks was a member of the Black Women's Political Council, a group determined to challenge segregation in court. After Parks's arrest the Council called for a citywide boycott of buses timed to begin the day of her trial. Since most riders of Montgomery's buses were black, their refusal to ride the vehicles was going to hurt business. Montgomery's black citizens hoped to use their economic leverage to force the city's bus company to change its policies. Within a few days the Black Women's Political Council coordinated its efforts with Montgomery's clergymen, who spread word of the boycott at the pulpit. As enthusiasm for the boycott spread, a new group was formed to organize it. The twenty-six-year-old King became its head.

King and others looked in amazement at the nearly empty buses that rolled down city streets the first morning of the boycott, December 5, 1955. For the next month and a half the boycott was so successful that the bus company complained it would soon run out of money. Eager to help the cause, Thurgood Marshall took the Montgomery bus case to federal court to challenge the city's segregation laws. When he won the case, Alabama officials appealed the decision to the Supreme Court. On November 13, 1956, the Supreme court ruled that Montgomery's segregation was unconstitutional. The jubilant African-American community of Montgomery ended their boycott in victory.

Though Marshall himself celebrated the results of the Montgomery reform efforts, he could not bring himself to approve the tactics used. As always, he believed that change should be made through the courts, not in the streets. For his cautious attitude concerning the civil rights movement, Marshall got criticized by many of King's followers, and later by the more militant reformers who succeeded King.

Marshall's critical words got lost in the wave of enthusiasm for nonviolent protest that swept the country in the 1960s. One of the most popular tactics was the sit-in. By that method people who wanted to end segregation in a store, restaurant, or other public area just sat on the premises until their demands got attention. The first sit-in to get national publicity took place in Greensboro, North Carolina.

On February 1, 1960, the year John F. Kennedy got elected president, four black university students walked into a Woolworth store in the college town of Greensboro. They bought school supplies and then sat down at the lunch counter to order coffee and doughnuts. They never got served. Instead the white waitress gestured in the direction of the hot dog stand set up for black customers in the basement. Refusing to budge, the students sat at the counter until closing time. Their spontaneous act of defiance touched off an onslaught of similar protests.

Marshall's disapproval of the tactic did not stop him from bringing the full weight of Fund, Inc., to support sit-in demonstrators. At a conference in March he set forth the organization's master plan to defend sit-ins in the courts. "If a dime store is open to the public," he told his audience, "anyone who enters is entitled to the same service anyone else gets. The right of protest is part of our tradition. It goes back to the tea dumped in Boston Harbor."

The following year Marshall took on the case of sixteen black students who staged sit-ins at a lunch counter and bus terminal in Baton Rouge, Louisiana. Found guilty of disturbing the peace by Louisiana courts, the students were fined and given thirty-day jail sentences. Marshall appealed the verdict to the Supreme Court. He and other Fund lawyers argued that the Louisiana convictions violated not only the Fourteenth Amendment but the First Amendment's guarantee of freedom of expression as well. The justices agreed and, in their opinion for *Garner v. Louisiana*, gave Marshall his last Supreme Court victory as head of Fund, Inc.

In the years 1960 and 1961 Marshall got the chance to make several trips related to the recent independence of African nations. In 1960 he flew to London to take part in a conference that drafted Kenya's constitution. A year later in April he served as President Kennedy's personal representative at the independence ceremonies of Sierra Leone in West Africa. Shortly after returning from this trip he received welcome news: President Kennedy wanted him to be a federal judge in one of the most prestigious courts in the nation—the Second Circuit Court of Appeals in New York City. Federal courts of appeals are divided into eleven circuits, or geographic regions. The Second Circuit covers the states of New York, Connecticut, and Vermont. It reviews about four hundred cases a year.

Since federal appeals courts are the highest in the legal system next to the Supreme Court, the Senate must scrutinize the record of each proposed judge before granting its approval. The branch of the Senate that confirms the presidential appointees is the Judiciary Committee. Its process of review is an important part of the balance of powers among the executive, judicial, and legislative branches of government. Yet, important as they are to ensure fairness in the system, the committee's hearings very often turn into political battles between Republicans and Democrats, and liberals and conservatives. Unfortunately for Marshall, judicial hearings on his appointment proved to be no exception. In 1961 the civil rights attorney who had so angered conservatives in the South was sub-

AP/WIDE WORLD PHOTOS

Marshall shakes the hand of Kenya's leader, Jomo Kenyatta, in Nairobi, 1963. The two men met to discuss civil rights. Marshall played an important role in drafting Kenya's constitution after independence.

jected to fierce questioning by several Southern senators, who found his record too radical. Wielding an enormous amount of political power, the Southerners held up his confirmation for eight months.

Finally, after getting approval, Marshall took up his post at the federal court in lower Manhattan in September 1962. Finding work as a judge very different from his former action-packed career, he admitted to his wife that he missed the excitement. One problem was that his fellow judges, quiet and formal, kept their office doors closed. The outgoing Marshall always kept his open. His secretary told reporters that he often seemed lonely. The second drawback of the job was that, as a freshman member of the court, Marshall was not assigned the most challenging cases. During his four-year tenure on the court he wrote 118 opinions, but most of them dealt with maritime law, labor disputes, patents and trademarks, and personal injuries—subjects in which Marshall was not very experienced. Still, his opinions were good enough so that not one was reversed on appeal to the Supreme Court.

In one case, though, Marshall dealt with issues a little closer to his heart. *Keyishian v. Board of Regents* centered around Professor Harry Keyishian and several colleagues who refused to sign a standard oath at their university pledging that they had never been affiliated with the Communist party. In his opinion Marshall stated that loyalty oaths violated the Fourteenth Amendment. Eventually, when the case reached the Supreme Court, the justices agreed with Marshall's opinion.

Marshall focused on the difficult task of being a judge, but he also stayed attuned to the explosive events that took place during Kennedy's brief tenure as president. During those years King and other black leaders stepped up their pressure for change. Mass rallies and protest movements were the order of the day, supported by a battery of lawsuits filed by Fund, Inc. For the first time in his career Marshall was not at the forefront of the struggle.

In 1961 black leaders launched "Freedom Riders," a campaign to desegregate buses. Relying on the methods of civil disobedience, blacks and whites alike boarded buses and sat in restricted seats. The Freedom Riders eventually met with success, but at great cost. In Montgomery, Alabama, Governor Wallace refused to protect the riders against an angry white mob. The violence reached such a pitch that President Kennedy was forced to dispatch four hundred federal marshals to the scene. Encouraged by the success of the Freedom Riders campaign, King organized massive demonstrations in Birmingham, Alabama, two years later. The televised images of Birmingham's police brutality sent shock waves across the nation. As a result Kennedy looked into formulating much-needed civil rights legislation.

Hoping to push Kennedy into signing a civil rights bill, King led hundreds of thousands of demonstrators in a march on Washington in August 1963. In front of an exuberant crowd King delivered the eloquent plea that went down in history. "I have a dream," he bellowed, "that my four little children will one day live in a nation where they will not be judged by the color of their skin but by the content of their character. I have a dream today!" Moved by King's words, President Kennedy got to work on civil rights legislation he never saw to completion. On November 22 the popular president was assassinated in Dallas, Texas, and his vice president, Lyndon Baines Johnson, assumed the seat of power. It was now up to Johnson to carry through on the Constitution's promise of equality.

9

Solicitor General of the United States

PRESIDENT JOHNSON PROVED to be a shrewd politician and, over the objections of Southern congressmen, ushered through the 1964 Civil Rights Act. The long-sought bill came ten years after *Brown v. Board of Education*, at a time when 90 percent of African-American children in the South and border states were still in all-black schools.

Johnson's civil rights bill brought welcome change in several areas. It outlawed segregation in such public places as hotels, theaters, parks, and swimming pools. It also gave the federal government increased power to enforce desegregation through the courts. The bill fell short, though, in the area of voting procedure, a continued source of discrimination against African-Americans. Obstructionist tactics used since the Civil War still kept them from the polls. In Alabama, for example, only five percent of eligible blacks were registered to vote.

Angered by the lack of progress, King and other leaders launched the 1964 "Freedom Summer," which sent volunteers through the South to register voters. The Freedom Summer campaign and several large demonstrations prompted Johnson to introduce strong voting-rights legislation in Congress. The same month, Congress passed a resolution that ensured U.S. military involvement in the Vietnam War. The 1960s were on their way to becoming the legendary decade of tumult.

As the voting-rights bill neared passage in July 1965, Marshall shared lunch with a few colleagues in the judges' private dining room at federal court. During the course of the meal he was interrupted by an assistant, who whispered that the president was on the phone. Puzzled, Marshall asked the aide, "The president of what?" The aide answered, "The president of the United States." Few federal judges ever received phone calls from the president. Marshall's surprise turned to amazement when he discovered what the call was about. Johnson wanted Marshall to become the country's next solicitor general, the top-ranking trial lawyer for the U.S. government. He asked Marshall to come to Washington to talk it over.

Deciding whether or not to take the job was not simple for Marshall. Though prestigious, the position would require him to give up a lifetime tenure as federal judge. His future as solicitor general would not be secure. Subject to the wishes of the president, it would most likely end when Johnson left office. Secondly, though far less important to Marshall, the job involved a cut in salary, from $33,000 a year to $28,500.

On the positive side, the post of solicitor general would allow Marshall to use his considerable talents as a lawyer. As Uncle Sam's attorney, he would argue the government's position before the Supreme Court and decide which cases to appeal to the Court. Marshall described the solicitor general's office as "the best law firm in the United States." The third-ranking lawyer in the land, Marshall would report only to the attorney general and his assistant, both of whom were known to give the solicitor general a free hand in designing legal strategy. Finally, the post would bring Marshall back into contact with the most pressing issues of the day. The Department of Justice had been given the green light to enforce both the Civil Rights and the Voting Rights acts, just passed by Congress. Once again, Marshall would have the opportunity to act as a general on his own turf.

What clinched the decision for the civil rights advocate was Johnson's wholehearted support for placing African-Americans in top government posts. Johnson hired more African-Americans for such posts than any president before him. Marshall felt it was his duty to support the chief executive in this effort. When asked by a reporter why he accepted the job, Marshall replied that it was "because the president asked me to." He went on to say, "I believe that in this time, especially, we do what our government requests of us. Negroes have made great advances in government, and I think it's time they started making some sacrifices."

This time Marshall's Senate confirmation went so smoothly that the entire procedure lasted only half an hour. A few days later, on August 24, the new solicitor general was sworn into office. Attending the ritual were, among others, NAACP executive Roy Wilkins; Marshall's sons, William and Thurgood, Jr.; his wife,

Cissy Marshall; and President Johnson. Afterward Johnson brought everyone into his office and heaped souvenirs on the two Marshall boys.

On October 11 the solicitor general participated in another ceremony in which he was formally presented to the Supreme Court. For the occasion Marshall wore the attire required of the solicitor general whenever he appeared before the justices. A holdover from the nineteenth century, the outfit consisted of dark-striped pants, a striped tie, a gray vest, and a cutaway coat that was short in front and reached down to his knees in back. The only article that seemed to be missing was a top hat. Marshall, who derided all pomp and formality, quipped to a reporter, "Now, isn't this the silliest getup in the world?"

Though he now occupied one of the most powerful offices in Washington, Marshall carried his down-home opinions with him. People who visited the solicitor general at the Department of Justice were struck by the contrast between the formality of the office and the easygoing man who occupied it. The office's high ceilings gave it a sense of grandeur. Ornate sculpted figures graced its powder-blue walls. The decor failed to impress Marshall, however. During his first few days on the job he was more concerned that the television didn't work. At one point he burst into an aide's office and asked, "How the hell do you work that noise box in my office? I can't get the World Series anywhere!" The press was generally favorable to the new solicitor general. Noting Marshall's fresh approach to his position, a reporter from *The New York Times* described him as "a genial fellow . . . with the generous wit of a born storyteller." As an attorney, moreover,

Marshall was less interested in the fine points of law than in the "human side" of his cases.

Indeed, Marshall's human side was put to the test immediately with a flood of civil rights cases. King remained at the helm of an increasingly popular movement. Activists denouncing U.S. involvement in the Vietnam War were gearing up for major demonstrations around the country. Added to their protests were the voices of angry city dwellers unwilling to endure poverty in silence. Only two days after Marshall's appointment as solicitor general, bloody race riots broke out in Watts, a section of Los Angeles that had become a dense urban ghetto. The problems faced by the North's slums exploded into view as riots broke out in major cities across America.

One of the first cases from the civil rights struggle to reach Marshall's desk was *United States v. Price*, dealing with the murder of three Freedom Riders in Mississippi. In July 1964 the bullet-ridden bodies of a black volunteer named James Chaney and his two white colleagues were uncovered by FBI agents in Philadelphia, Mississippi. After that the FBI led police to the murderers. Of the eighteen people suspected of the crime—including Philadelphia's Sheriff Rainey—only seven were held. All of them were treated as heroes by the white community.

Even though agents of the U.S. government had pinpointed the murder suspects, the government had no authority to prosecute them. Because of the separation of state and federal powers, the federal government may not press murder charges against citizens for crimes committed in a state. Marshall and others at the Department of Justice had to come up with other grounds on which to snag the suspects. They found those grounds in the U.S. Constitution. Since Chaney and his fellow volunteers had been working to secure voting rights, Marshall and other Justice officials said the murder suspects had obstructed the civil rights of U.S. citizens, a federal crime. They ordered a Mississippi federal court to try the suspects on that ground. Eventually the men were found guilty and received the maximum sentences of three to ten years. The case marked the first time that an all-white Southern jury sentenced fellow whites in a civil rights case.

In other civil rights cases the solicitor general tackled issues of desegregation. Taking the side of African-Americans in *Evans v. Newton*, Marshall sent a brief to the Supreme Court arguing that a private park in Macon, Georgia, served a "public function" and should be open to blacks and whites alike. The Court agreed and ordered the park desegregated. In *Reitman v. Mulkey* Marshall informed the Court of the government's strong support of fair housing laws in California.

Like the Civil Rights Act, the 1965 Voting Rights Act instructed federal courts to take an active role in promoting the new legislation. They were to direct their decisions in favor of voter registration and fair practices at the polls. To make the courts' job easier, the law expressly outlawed literacy tests and other discriminatory devices favored in the South. As expected, the Southern states most affected by the Voting Rights Act chafed under its provisions and sought the earliest opportunity to challenge it in court. With this goal in mind, South Carolina brought suit against the U.S. attorney general in a 1965 case titled *South*

Carolina v. Katzenbach. Defying government interference in its affairs once again, South Carolina argued that in passing the Voting Rights Act, the U.S. government had overstepped its authority. Moreover, South Carolina complained that it was being singled out by the government for unfair treatment.

In his brief supporting the attorney general's position, Marshall argued that the Voting Rights Act was upheld by the Fifteenth Amendment, adopted in 1870. That amendment, which secured the right to vote for African-Americans, also gave Congress the power "to enforce this legislation."

After considering both Marshall's brief and the oral arguments of Attorney General Katzenbach, the Supreme Court issued a unanimous opinion in favor of the new legislation. Speaking for the Court, Chief Justice Earl Warren delivered a stirring endorsement of the rights of African-Americans. "After enduring nearly a century of widespread resistance to the Fifteenth Amendment, Congress has marshaled an array of potent weapons against the evil. . . . Hopefully, millions of non-white Americans will now be able to participate for the first time on an equal basis in the government under which they live."

Emboldened by the Court's stance on equal rights at the polls, Marshall went on to argue the winning side in several other voting cases. The first, *Katzenbach v. Morgan*, arose in the state of New York, where many Puerto Ricans were forbidden to vote because they could not read, write, or speak English. Citing "invidious discrimination," the Supreme Court ruled favorably on Marshall's brief, which argued for giving non-English-speaking people the right to vote.

Soon afterward Marshall took on a case challenging

117

the legality of the poll tax. For centuries Virginia had levied a tax on anyone who wanted to vote in elections. This practice kept many poor people from casting a ballot. The Twenty-fourth Amendment had expressly outlawed this procedure for federal elections in 1964, but it said nothing about local and state elections. In 1965 several African-American residents of Virginia contested the taxes in federal court. In ruling against the African-Americans, Virginia's federal judges stated that local and state elections were under Virginia's sole jurisdiction.

As *Harper v. Board of Elections* made its way to the Supreme Court, the stage was set for another contest of power between state and federal government. In this case, like many others Marshall handled, the U.S. government was not a direct party in the suit, even though its interests were at stake. In these instances the solicitor general got the government's point of view across in a "friend of the court" brief, or *amicus curiae* as it is called in Latin. *Amicus curiae* briefs, especially those coming from the government, take on great significance at the Court.

In his *amicus* brief Marshall asserted that poll taxes violated the Fourteenth Amendment. He also pointed to the parts of the Constitution covering elections to argue that the state's authority to regulate voting procedure does not extend to "unbridled license to exclude any citizens from the electoral process that it may choose." Though not united in its opinion, the Court agreed with Marshall's line of thinking. It voted six to three to favor Virginia's black citizens. Speaking for the majority, William O. Douglas stated, "Wealth, like race, creed, or color, is not germane [relevant] to one's ability to participate intelligently in the electoral process.''

In addition to civil rights matters, the solicitor general dealt with a wide range of issues. He took on, among others, cases involving corporate mergers, labor-management relations, tax evasion, and the deportation of aliens. Among his most publicized, however, were the cases related to government wiretapping. As the power of FBI director J. Edgar Hoover had grown, so had the agency's installation of listening devices in private homes and offices. Marshall insisted that such devices violated a citizen's right to privacy, guaranteed in the Fourth Amendment. Addressing a meeting of the Association of Federal Investigators, he warned those present that the "evil" of electronic eavesdropping would not be tolerated in the courts.

In *Black v. United States* he successfully argued that evidence obtained by illegal wiretapping could not be used in court testimony. His position concerning wiretapping earned him a reputation for being too hard on the government and soft on criminals. But in the later *Hoffa v. United States* he upheld the government's right to use informants in criminal prosecutions. Generally, though, Marshall staunchly defended the rights of the accused. Through the years he supported the famous *Miranda* ruling (*Miranda v. Arizona*, 1966) that held, among other things, that suspects must be informed of their rights at the time of arrest.

Though Marshall often endured criticism from liberals and conservatives, he never let it affect his strong views. When the civil rights advocate seized on a moral issue, he was relentless in pushing it through the courts. Commenting on this trait, his assistant at the Department of Justice said, "He can be tough with those who oppose or cross him." He had no sympathy for the views of those who accused the Supreme Court of going too far to protect civil rights. Delivering a speech at the University of Miami in 1966, he scorned his critics for their refusal "to shake free of nineteenth-century moorings."

Marshall's singular drive in pushing for social reform did not carry over to efforts at self-improvement. Before he was forced to quit because of a heart attack in 1967, he smoked up to three packs of cigarettes a day. He was also incautious about his weight. In 1967 a *New York Times* reporter described his hefty frame—six feet two inches and 210 pounds—as that of a football player. In the same year, though, another reporter commented that excessive weight was beginning to show on "a man whose idea of physical exercise is to avoid all thoughts of it." Years of desk jobs were taking their toll on the fifty-seven-year-old attorney. Though Cissy Marshall badgered him to exercise, he successfully avoided her advice for years. The one outdoor activity he took part in was playing touch football with his children. Otherwise he played the spectator, watching sports on TV and accompanying the boys to Redskins games.

By now the family was settled in a comfortable townhouse at 64 G Street in Capital Park, an integrated neighborhood in Southwest Washington. Thurgood, Jr., and William were enrolled at the Georgetown Day School. When not working, Marshall joined Cissy in entertaining some of the top personalities in Washington. To relax, the solicitor general listened to jazz and classical music and watched his favorite Westerns on TV, "still waiting to see one showing where the Indians win." The former Baltimorean also liked to cook Southern dishes for friends. His Baltimore-style she-crab soup was much admired, as were his pig-feet special, praised by his friend Lena Horne as the best in the world. "I can do anything but pastry," he proudly admitted.

Marshall's life would have continued on its keel were it not for the fact that President Johnson had other plans in store for him. In June 1967 Johnson once again summoned Marshall to his office for an urgent conference. This time it was to tell the solicitor general that he was being appointed to serve as a justice of the U.S. Supreme Court.

10

Justice Thurgood Marshall

SHORTLY BEFORE NOON on July 13, 1967, Marshall stood in the hot sun of the White House Rose Garden. While reporters took notes and clicked their cameras, TV technicians rolled their film for the national news networks. Blinking in the midday light, President Johnson stepped up to the microphone to make his surprise announcement: Thurgood Marshall was his choice to be the ninety-sixth justice of the Supreme Court. "I believe he has already earned his place in history," Johnson told the crowd, adding, "I believe it is the right thing to do, the right time to do it, the right man, and the right place."

Reaction to the announcement was swift. Martin Luther King, Jr., hailed Marshall for being "the legal champion of the Negro revolution." Floyd B. Mc-Kissick, head of the Congress of Racial Equality (CORE) said, "This has stirred pride in the breast of every black American." Echoing these sentiments was Joseph D. Tydings, senator from Maryland, who told the press, "Today is a proud day for Maryland. For the first time since the Civil War, when Roger B. Taney was Chief Justice, [Maryland] shall be represented on the nation's highest bench.''

What Tydings neglected to mention, however, was the fact that Chief Justice Taney presided over the infamous *Dred Scott* decision. In 1857 Taney and the other justices ruled that African-American slaves and former slaves were ''property,'' and not citizens under the U.S. Constitution, which was made ''for whites by whites.'' Obviously the Supreme Court had made great progress since that time. The early justices never would have imagined that the great-grandson of a slave could one day serve on the Court. ''Even twenty years ago, such an appointment would have been inconceivable,'' the *Washington Post* reported.

Yet not every reaction to the African-American Supreme Court nominee was positive. Marshall's appointment incurred the wrath of die-hard Southern traditionalists and their representatives in the Senate. They were sure to give him a rough time in the upcoming Senate confirmation hearings. Marshall had already received a taste of how difficult the process could be in 1961, when the Senate held up his confirmation for eight long months. He wondered what would happen now that the political stakes were higher. He knew that the Judiciary Committee hearings often turned into partisan battles. After all, the Senate had blocked 21 out of the 124 Supreme Court appointments ever made—nearly 20 percent of them. Years later Marshall's successor, Clarence Thomas, would go through a grueling Senate confirmation battle as difficult as his own.

Marshall did not have to wait long to test the temperature of the Senate. With Cissy Marshall by his side on July 13, he began the five intense days of questioning before a sixteen-man committee. New York's senator Jacob Javits opened the session by praising Marshall as "one of the most distinguished lawyers in the land." But soon questions were fired by Southern senators who tried to prove that Marshall was too soft on crime. The Supreme Court nominee politely declined to answer many of their inquiries because they dealt with issues he would have to confront on the Court. It is well known that the justices do not discuss their ideas on upcoming cases in public. Refusing to give up on their line of attack, though, senators McClellan and Ervin probed Marshall's controversial opinions on wiretapping, confessions, and a suspect's right to consult a lawyer. "I'm as worried as anybody about the mounting rate of crime," Marshall told the senators. "But I am equally determined that whatever is to be done must be done within [the framework of] the United States Constitution."

Next Senator Strom Thurmond of South Carolina subjected the nominee to an hour-long quiz on constitutional history and law. Rattling off sixty questions, he asked Marshall about such things as the "black codes" of the nineteenth century and the names of the congressional committee members who drafted post–Civil War amendments. Marshall was unable to answer most of the questions, to the delight of his interrogator. Later, when the committee presented its findings to the full Senate, a triumphant Thurmond told the room that Marshall couldn't even name the men who drafted the Fourteenth Amendment. Coming to Marshall's defense, Senator Edward Kennedy of Massachusetts asked Thurmond if he could come up with the names himself. Unable to do so, the ruffled senator promptly ended his harangue.

Fortunately Thurmond's fellow senators were swayed less by Marshall's inability to answer difficult questions than by his measured and dignified testimony. In a vote of 69 to 11, they gave him resounding approval.

One month later, on October 2, 1967, the Supreme Court welcomed its new associate justice (often the word *associate* is dropped from the title). The inaugural ceremony took place in the Court's central chamber. Seated next to President Johnson were Marshall's wife and sons; his brother, Aubrey, now a successful surgeon in Delaware; and other guests. For the swearing-in Marshall placed his hand on the Bible and swore to "administer justice without respect to persons, and do equal right to the poor and to the rich." Missing from the proud onlookers that day were Marshall's parents, both of whom had died. The new associate justice said, though, that he was sure his father was on some street corner in heaven shaking his finger and saying, "I knew my boy would do it."

Immediately after the ceremony Marshall took a seat behind the justices' bench and began work on the Court's term, which usually lasts from October to June or July. Observers thought Marshall would add a distinctly liberal voice to the Court. Marshall, though, refused to be pegged by categories. "I am not attached to any legal school of thought," he told a reporter. He quickly added, "But I am also not a conservative."

Most Supreme Court decisions demand a great deal of compromise from the justices, who often trade votes and influence like politicians. Six steps go into making a decision. First the justices meet weekly in a strictly private conference to select the cases they will consider. This process is called granting writs of *cer-*

tiori, or certs for short. Next oral arguments of the case are scheduled and heard. A few days after the last oral arguments the justices get together to discuss the case and take a preliminary vote.

One member of the majority is then assigned to write an opinion. Since the opinion incorporates the views of between five and nine justices, a lot of back-and-forth discussion takes place. Every member of the majority has to agree on the points being made. Often the work takes months and goes through several drafts. Court clerks, hired from among recent law-school graduates, provide valuable help in the research, writing, and circulation of opinions.

After the draft is passed around, the justices either join or reject the opinion. If they reject it, they have the opportunity to write a dissent giving their reasons for disagreement. Otherwise they can write a concurring opinion showing agreement with the final decision but giving different arguments for arriving at it. Once the opinion, which technically includes dissents and concurrences, is ready to be announced, the justices must agree once again on how much of it is to be made public and later published in official documents. Published opinions, including dissents and concurrences, affect the future course of law.

In the give-and-take of decision making, Marshall proved to be resilient, but he stubbornly stuck to his principles on a number of occasions. In one case, deciding the fate of a white baseball player who did not want to be traded, Marshall criticized his colleague's draft opinion. To prove a point in the opinion, Justice Harry Blackmun had entered statistics of the great baseball players of all time. They may be great, Marshall pointed out, but not one of the players Blackmun listed was black. The race of the players made no difference to the argument—Marshall just couldn't stand seeing a list of great players exclude blacks. Responding to Marshall's complaint, Blackmun hastily added Jackie Robinson, Roy Campanella, and Satchel Paige.

On other occasions Marshall doggedly upheld constitutional issues, especially in the area of discrimination. On questions regarding the Fourteenth Amendment, Marshall followed no one's opinions but his own. Otherwise, in decisions requiring a scholarly or technical grasp of the law, the new justice followed the lead of his admired friend Justice William Brennan. He sometimes scribbled "Follow Bill" on his instructions to clerks. Just two years older than Marshall, the small-framed, gregarious Brennan became his most trusted companion at the Court.

During his first term Marshall authored ten of the court's majority opinions. Three of them dealt with freedom of speech guaranteed under the First Amendment. One of the free-speech cases, *Pickering v. Board of Education*, dealt with an Illinois high school teacher who was fired for writing a letter to the local newspaper criticizing a decision taken by the school board. After the school board fired Pickering, the teacher sued to get his job back, but lost in Illinois state court. Thanks to Marshall and the other justices who delivered an opinion reversing the lower court's opinion, Pickering went back to work. As U.S. citizens, Marshall wrote, teachers have the right to express their views on matters of public debate. In a later case Marshall upheld the free-speech rights of union members picketing a shopping-mall store. The First Amendment, he said, protects peaceful conduct as well as speech.

If Marshall was forceful in ensuring the rights of free speech, he was unwavering in his support for the rights of African-American schoolchildren. Marshall was angry that desegregation had not been enforced for the majority of students in the American school system. In the South alone only fifteen percent of black students attended nonsegregated schools. When school boards brought their pleas for delay to the Court, the man who had championed *Brown* showed little patience. Of all the justices he was the most outspoken in challenging school boards and their attorneys during oral arguments. At the hearings of *Green v. The School Board of New Kent County, Virginia*, Marshall told the attorneys he was appalled that "at this late date" county school officials had not complied with *Brown*. His phrase "at this late date" found its way into Justice Brennan's opinion, which ordered Kent County to desegregate without delay.

The Court's ruling in *Green* came during a time when race relations in the country had reached another boiling point. The previous year, on the day Marshall's appointment to the Supreme Court had been announced, newspapers carried headlines about terrible race riots in Tampa and Cincinnati. On the same day *The New York Times* carried a cover story about the dismal education received by African-American students in Detroit's inner city, an area that typified America's urban problems. As pressure both for and against reform mounted, the country was shocked to hear, on April 4, 1968, that Rev. Martin

Luther King, Jr., had been gunned down by an assassin outside his Georgia motel.

With his death, the peaceful campaign for reform seemed to come to an end. Into King's place strode younger and more militant leaders who had been gaining strength since the mid-1960s. The new militants, some of whom supported the use of violence to achieve their ends, found fault with Marshall for working within the legal system. The longtime advocate of "freedom through law" openly criticized much of the protest that swept American universities in the 1960s. He believed that many of the protesters were poorly informed of the issues. But he was more alarmed by their readiness to resort to violence. In a speech delivered to university students in New Orleans on May 4, 1969, Marshall said, "It takes no courage to get in the back of a crowd and throw a rock. Rather, it takes courage to stand up on your own two feet and look anyone straight in the eye and say 'I will not be beaten.'"

Once, Marshall was accused by a student of not being "militant enough." The student wanted to know why Marshall had not marched with Martin Luther King, Jr., and others in demonstrations in such places as Selma, Alabama. Referring to the fact that his civil rights campaign in the South began long before the 1960s, Marshall told the young man, "I was there before you were born." To another student with a similar complaint, he said, "I was in Selma. Not with a whole lot of troops protecting me. I was there with nobody but a lawyer from Birmingham and me, all by our lonesome in a car, at a time when [your] father was too scared to move out of the house."

Soon Marshall's views came under attack from the opposite end of the political spectrum. In November 1968 the conservative Republican Richard M. Nixon was elected president. Nixon's election brought an end to eight years of Democratic rule and the presidency of Lyndon Johnson. The plainspoken Johnson had done more for the rights of African-Americans than any president before him. "I loved that man," Marshall admitted later. During Johnson's administration Marshall not only reached the pinnacle of his career but also acted as a government representative on several trips to Africa. In 1965 he flew to Kenya to discuss civil rights with the nation's leader, Jomo Kenyatta. Two years later the associate justice was sent on an eight-nation tour of Africa.

Instead of a political mentor and ally, Marshall now faced a strong critic in Richard Nixon. Opposed to the climate of the Court, which he found too liberal, Nixon vowed to change it. In his plan "caretakers of the Constitution" would replace the "super legislators" of the Court. Within a few months of his inauguration Nixon appointed Warren Burger to replace the retiring Earl Warren as chief justice. Burger was known for his conservative, law-and-order views.

The 1968–69 Court term, Earl Warren's last, resulted in a landmark decision in the area of free speech. The decision, *Stanley v. Georgia*, dealt with the arrest of a Georgia resident for possession of three films judged obscene by police officers who entered his home. In his opinion overturning the conviction, Marshall revealed strong views on the subject: "If the First Amendment means anything, it means that a state has no business telling a man, sitting alone in his house, what books he may read or what films he may watch. Our whole constitutional heritage rebels at the thought of giving Government the power to control men's minds."

Later in the term the associate justice ruled on an issue he found increasingly vital—the rights of the accused. In *Benton v. Maryland*, 1969, Marshall upheld the Fifth Amendment's guarantee against "double jeopardy," being tried twice for the same crime. Marshall said that any state that ignores the ban on double jeopardy denies its citizens their rights.

Throughout his years on the Court, Marshall never let his distinguished position alter his down-to-earth style. His usual lunch was a can of soup he ate at his desk, and he got his hair cut at the local barbershop for $3.50. Unlike several justices who kept their distance from the clerks, Marshall invited them to his house to talk and shoot pool. With the other justices Marshall was friendly and talkative. His lively way with words earned him the title of Court storyteller.

Underneath Marshall's friendliness lay an acute awareness of his being the only African-American among the justices. He once told a reporter, "What do they know about Negroes? . . . Sure, they went to school with *one* Negro in the class. Name one who lives in a neighborhood with Negroes." Occasionally he used his difference from the others to humorous effect. He liked to surprise Chief Justice Burger in the hallways with the greeting, "What's shakin', Chief baby?"

His favorite prank involved duping tourists who mistook him for the elevator operator as they stepped into the justices' private elevator. When the unsuspecting riders called for "First floor, please," Marshall slipped into Southern attitude and dialogue. "Yowsa,

yowsa," he responded, while going through the motions of operating the fully automated elevator. When the elevator reached its destination, he held the door for the passengers, enjoying their astonishment when they realized who he was.

Balancing his humor and diplomacy with a strong inner conviction, Marshall adjusted to his first few years on the Court with ease. Soon, though, he encountered potent resistance to his ideals. With the addition of three Nixon-appointed associate justices in 1970 and 1971, the Court began a long slide into conservatism. Favoring the status quo over change, and reversing several opinions close to Marshall's heart, his fellow justices turned adversarial on many issues. Responding to difficulty as he had in the past, Marshall continued the uphill fight for "freedom through law" for the next two decades.

11

A Legacy of Hope

LIKE THE STORMY decade that preceded it, the 1970s proved to be a tumultuous one for Marshall and the justices on the Supreme Court. Because of their decisions on a number of heated issues, the Supreme Court justices were hurled into the center of controversy. In 1971, over the objections of the U.S. government, they allowed *The New York Times* to publish a sensitive government document concerning the Vietnam War. Then, in 1972, the justices supported a woman's right to make her own choice about abortion in *Roe v. Wade*.

The most volatile issue facing the nation in the 1970s, however, was busing. To speed up desegregation, the Court had ruled that black children could be bused to white schools and white children to black schools. Then in 1971 the justices agreed to hear a busing case called *Swann v. The Charlotte-Mecklenburg Board of Education*, which caused an uproar.

The case had come to the Court on appeal from a federal court in North Carolina. Responding to complaints from black parents in Mecklenburg County, a federal judge had directed the county to desegregate its schools, using busing as a major tool. Furthermore he ordered each school to create a ratio of blacks to whites that reflected the balance of the county's population. To achieve this, he said, the county would have to alter its school zoning policies. Calling the plan too drastic, the school board took the case to a federal appeals court and won. The black parents then brought the case to the Supreme Court.

The idea of busing irritated President Nixon, who had just issued a policy statement saying that children should attend their neighborhood schools. His statement ignored the problems brought about by residential segregation (the separation of whites and blacks into different neighborhoods). In fact, many segregated neighborhoods were deliberately zoned to keep white children in white schools and black children in black schools. As the population in poor, urban Southern neighborhoods swelled, an increasing number of black children found themselves stuck in inferior, segregated schools.

The national debate on the issue found its counterpart in the chambers of the Supreme Court. Like Nixon, Justice Burger felt that busing went too far. The chief justice opposed segregation, but felt that uprooting children from their neighborhoods to achieve a population balance was beyond the scope of *Brown*. There was a difference, he said, between desegregation and integration. Integration implied strict racial balance between blacks and whites. He felt the Court should be concerned only with desegregation, striking down policies that keep schools entirely one race.

Disagreeing with Burger were justices Brennan, Marshall, and Douglas, who championed integration.

134

They believed that predominantly black schools, whether brought about by law or by residential segregation, damaged students' self-image and motivation. Since they realized that it would take too long to correct residential segregation, they opted for busing as the best immediate solution. At the same time the three allies were eager to work with the other justices in forming a unanimous opinion in the *Swann* case. They knew that disagreement among the justices on the crucial issue of busing would send the wrong signal to school boards everywhere.

No one was more aware of this need for unanimity than Marshall. Though he held strong views on the subject, he was willing to make a few concessions so that the Court could show a united front. With this goal in mind, the pragmatic associate justice gave in on a few points in the final opinion. He insisted, though, that the opinion underscore the clear message that residential segregation had to end. In this case he was willing to lose a scuffle if he could go on to win the war.

As the result of compromise by Marshall and the other justices, the Supreme Court was able to come up with a unanimous opinion in *Swann v. The Charlotte-Mecklenburg Board of Education*. In 1971 they ruled in favor of the black parents who wanted their children bused to school. Though the justices did not agree with every point the lower federal-court judge had made in the *Swann* case, they approved his idea of correcting residential imbalances in school enrollment. Busing won its strongest case to date.

The next busing case to come before the Supreme Court dealt with the long-smoldering issue of segregation in the North. The South's school segregation had been *de jure*, meaning that it came about through laws. But in the North, *de facto*, or actual, segregation was brought about by population pressures and lack of jobs, which forced more and more African-Americans into the cities. There, they found themselves confined to ghettos. Urban poverty reached into every area of their lives, including public schools, which were understaffed and badly equipped. For inner-city children the defeat of "separate but equal" had made little difference. Their problems had less to do with segregation than with the poor funding their schools received.

Making matters worse for these children were the discriminatory practices of landlords, school boards, and other officials that intensified residential segregation. Detroit, like many other cities in the North and West, showed a bull's-eye pattern of residential segregation. Blacks occupied the core of the city, surrounded by rings of white suburbs. Moreover, bias against blacks in Detroit's school-zoning policies had created a system of busing that sent whites to white schools and blacks to black schools, even when white ones were closer.

In the early 1970s a group of black parents in Detroit became fed up with sending their kids to inferior schools. They decided to challenge the zoning system in court. In *Milliken v. Bradley* they sued the state of Michigan for dividing Detroit's school zoning along strictly racial lines. In federal court the judges reacted to the parents' complaint by ruling that Detroit had to integrate its schools. The judges then announced their far-reaching plan to bus students between the city and the suburbs. The black parents who brought the suit were elated, but white parents were enraged and became active in opposing the decision. Several black parents were bothered by it as well. They were afraid at the thought of sending their children far away to white, and potentially hostile, suburbs. Several of them believed that there was nothing wrong with all-black city schools, providing they got adequate funding.

By the time *Milliken v. Bradley* reached the Supreme Court, in 1974, the justices were under antibusing pressure from the Nixon administration. In a 1972 speech President Nixon had attacked not only busing but desegregation as well. Moreover, Nixon's three appointees to the Court were making it clear that they supported the president's views. After a lot of heated discussion the three of them joined Chief Justice Burger's majority opinion striking down Detroit's busing plan. They upheld the right to bus children within towns and cities but rejected the idea of busing between cities and suburbs.

Marshall, who saw the Michigan federal-court ruling as a bellwether of progress, was infuriated by the Supreme Court's decision. In a dissenting opinion he denounced the "giant step backward." "In the short run," he warned, "it may seem to be the easiest course to allow our great metropolitan areas to be divided up into two cities—one white, the other black—but it is a course, I predict, our people will ultimately regret." His sentiments were echoed later by sociologists who pointed to the increasing isolation and deterioration of America's inner cities.

If Marshall was upset by the defeat in *Milliken*, he was more alarmed by the conservative backslide in a case involving affirmative action four years later. The landmark case, *Regents of the University of Califor-*

nia v. Bakke, 1978, affected the hiring of minorities and their admission into schools. It started when a white medical-school applicant named Alan Bakke got rejected by the University of California in favor of a minority candidate. In rejecting Bakke, the university had followed a relatively new quota system. Through this plan officials made up for past discrimination by assigning a specific number of places, called quotas, to minority applicants. Claiming the plan unfair, Bakke sued the university on grounds of reverse discrimination.

Marshall saw quotas as a temporary remedy for the racial and ethnic imbalances in schools, corporations, and government offices. His fellow justices, however, did not. In 1978 they ruled that Bakke was right—quotas discriminated against mainstream candidates. The majority opinion in *Bakke* incorporated the vote of the Court's newest member, John Paul Stevens, a conservative appointed by Republican president Gerald Ford. His voice replaced the staunchly liberal one of William O. Douglas, Marshall's strong ally who retired. Now Marshall and Brennan stood alone on many civil rights issues.

As Marshall's influence on the Court weakened, his voice grew more strident. Attacking *Bakke*'s ban on quotas, he wrote, "The experience of Negroes in America has been different in kind, not just in degree, from that of other ethnic groups. It is not merely the history of slavery alone but also that a whole people were marked as inferior by the law. . . . The dream of America as the great melting pot has not been realized for the Negro." Later, in a speech delivered to Howard University students, he argued that equal opportunity for African-American youth had not yet been achieved. "These Negro kids are not fools," he told his audience. "They know when you tell them there is a possibility that someday they'll have a chance to be the O-N-L-Y Negro on the Supreme Court that those odds aren't too good."

Distressed by his colleagues' narrow interpretation of the Constitution in deciding affirmative action, busing, and other cases, Marshall set forth his own point of view about the great document. In 1987 he delivered a sharp critique of the founding fathers' sense of justice in a speech marking the 200th anniversary of the U.S. Constitution. "I do not believe that the meaning of the Constitution was forever 'fixed' at the Philadelphia Convention," the associate justice told his listeners. "Nor do I find the wisdom, foresight, and sense of justice exhibited by the framers particularly profound. To the contrary, the government they devised was defective from the start, requiring several amendments, a Civil War, and a momentous social transformation." He added that "the true miracle was not the birth of the Constitution but its life."

Holding out hope for a better future based on law, Marshall said, "[African-Americans] were enslaved by law, emancipated by law, disenfranchised and segregated by law, and finally, they have begun to win equality by law. Along the way new constitutional principles have emerged to meet the challenges of a changing society. This progress has been dramatic, and it will continue."

Later on, Marshall showed his characteristic humor when he talked to a reporter about the bicentennial festivities. The Supreme Court justices had received an unusual invitation to attend the reenactment of the Constitutional Convention of 1787, during which time the Constitution was drafted. "If you are going to do what you did two hundred years ago," Marshall quipped, "somebody is going to give me short pants and a tray so I can serve coffee."

Marshall knew, of course, that no one would ask him to serve coffee at that or any other meeting. On the contrary, during the last several decades he had been honored with special college degrees, awards, commemorative plaques, dedications of important buildings, and statues crafted in his likeness. In 1980 a nine-foot bronze statue of Marshall was installed in front of the Baltimore federal courthouse. The occasion marked the 100th anniversary of the Baltimore Bar Association, the prestigious lawyers' organization that had excluded black members when Marshall was a young attorney.

Speaking at the unveiling ceremony on May 16, the honored guest acknowledged the progress made in race relations, but warned that the nation still had a long way to go in this area. "Some Negroes feel we have arrived," Marshall told his listeners. "Others feel there is nothing more to do. I just want to be sure that when you see this statue, you won't think that's the end of it. I won't have it that way. There's too much to be done."

The artist who made the statue, Reuben Kramer, said the work was inspired by the fact that "Marshall grew from the slums of West Baltimore to the heights of the Supreme Court." Over the two years it took to complete the statue, Kramer and Marshall developed a warm relationship. "Marshall used to call me Brother Kramer," the white Baltimorean recalled, "and it was the greatest compliment I could have gotten." Kramer was struck by the justice's boundless energy. "He entered the room like a cannon," he remembered, "and never sat down."

Court observers wondered how long Marshall's energy would hold up. As the 1980s progressed, his health seriously deteriorated. A flock of reporters and political analysts began to make predictions about Marshall's retirement. The aging justice jokingly referred to this process as the "deathwatch" and stubbornly said he would live to be 110, "shot by a jealous husband." In a more serious vein he vowed he would not give up his Supreme Court seat during the tenure of a president who would fill it with a conservative. Marshall knew that a young replacement would influence the Court for decades.

Nonetheless, throughout Marshall's later years on the Court, the countdown continued. Once, there was a false report circulated that Marshall had died. On hearing the news, the chief justice's secretary called Mrs. Marshall to give her support and urge her to remain calm. "Well, I'm very calm," Cecilia Marshall told her caller, "because he's there in the living room having his dinner."

Throughout his later years Marshall's reputation swelled to great heights. In April 1991 *Separate But Equal*, a sweeping, four-hour docudrama depicting the eventful days surrounding *Brown v. Board of Education*, appeared on television. Playing Marshall in the lead role was Oscar-winning actor Sidney Poitier. Breaking his thirty-six-year avoidance of television acting in order to do the part, Poitier said, "I've never played anything as meaningful about my times as this." He called Marshall "a living legend." "Here was a man who could have taken his law degree and made a lot of money," the actor said, "but he had a point of view and a commitment that came out of a value system—and that best illustrates the man.''

The film came out at a crucial time for Marshall. Though proud of his life's accomplishments, he was far from satisfied with the status of African-Americans, who needed more help than ever. He was familiar with the disheartening statistics. One out of three African-Americans was mired in poverty. Six out of every ten African-American students never finished high school. Fifty-six years after Donald Murray was admitted to the University of Maryland, under 6 percent of American law students were black. Moreover the discrimination that affected African-Americans also hurt Hispanic-Americans, Asian-Americans, Native Americans, and women.

For much of the stalled progress in the rights of women and minority groups, Marshall laid the finger of blame on recent decisions of the Supreme Court. In an unusually outspoken article about the Court in 1990, Marshall listed defeats in the areas of affirmative action, job discrimination, free speech, and other vital areas. ''Power, not reason, is the new currency of this Court's decision making,'' Marshall told the press in 1991, referring to the Court's readiness to uphold the views of the Reagan and Bush administrations.

The issue that finally tipped the scales for the eighty-two-year-old justice, though, was the Court's handling of the rights of criminals and suspects. Marshall's dogged views on the matter prompted critics to attack him in the press. In 1989 *Fortune* magazine accused him of being ''soft on crime, riddled by liberal pieties, oblivious to the real-world problems of America's cops.'' His sympathy for suspects and convicts arose from the fact that he felt many of them were wrongly accused.

The aspect of criminal prosecution Marshall most strongly denounced was the death penalty. His fervent opposition to the practice grew out of his early experiences in the South and during his work with court-martial victims in the Korean War. He saw first-hand how racially prejudiced judges and juries could send the wrong people to their deaths. In Marshall's view the death penalty "wreaks havoc with our entire criminal justice system."

Thanks in part to Marshall's vote, the Supreme Court struck down the death penalty in 1968. But a more conservative court upheld it in 1976. At that time Marshall strongly disagreed with the reinstatement. Years later, in one of his last opinions, Marshall again delivered a passionate dissent denouncing the death penalty. In 1990 the Court sent convict Wilbert Lee Evans to his death in Virginia. Evans's execution marked the 141st to take place since 1976. Arguing the black convict's case as the lone dissenter among the justices, Marshall once again insisted that the Eighth Amendment prohibits "cruel and unusual punishment." Evans was so moved by Marshall's plea that he said he would take it with him to his grave.

That same year Marshall received another blow at the Supreme Court when Justice William Brennan retired. The departure of his longtime friend left Marshall isolated among a chorus of conservative voices. In late June 1991 those voices united to overrule two previous decisions concerning the rights of suspected criminals. As usual Marshall fired off two angry dissents. Two hours after delivering them in Court on June 28, the weary justice announced his retirement.

Citing health problems as the reason, he wrote his official letter of resignation to President Bush. Twenty-four years of service by one of the Court's greatest justices was brought to an abrupt end.

As news of Marshall's decision flashed across news desks and television sets, words of praise and regret flooded in to the Court. Civil rights leaders forecast the end of a progressive era. President Bush announced that Marshall had "rendered extraordinary and distinguished service to his country. His career is an inspiring example for all Americans." Republican senator Orrin Hatch said, "I don't know of anyone on the bench who has had a more profound effect on American jurisprudence."

Immediately following Marshall's announcement, President Bush appointed another African-American, Judge Clarence Thomas, to fill the vacancy on the Court. In the summer of 1991 Thomas emerged triumphant from bitter and widely publicized confirmation hearings during which he was accused of sexually harassing female colleagues at work. Most Court observers knew that Thomas's record on the Court would be very different from that of Marshall, especially since Thomas had openly attacked his predecessor's views on the Constitution.

Few people were prepared, though, for the extent of the differences that emerged. Within a few months Thomas dove into decisions that directly contradicted Marshall's opinions. In one case, involving a prisoner who was badly beaten by guards, Thomas argued that the prisoner was not protected by the Eighth Amendment. Because of this and other opinions *The New York Times* dubbed him "The Youngest, Cruelest Justice."

NATIONAL GEOGRAPHIC SOCIETY, COURTESY OF THE SUPREME COURT HISTORICAL SOCIETY

The Supreme Court justices, 1990 term. Justice Marshall is sitting fourth from left. Standing, second from left, is Justice Sandra Day O'Connor, the first woman justice.

Saddened by Thomas's effect on American law, Marshall continues to speak out against discrimination, human rights abuses, and the conservative drift of the Court. In January 1992 he served as a guest judge in New York City's Second Circuit Court of Appeals, his old haunt. The feisty Marshall had apparently lost none of his spirit. "I'm still alive," he joked to the journalists who gathered around him. Despite enormous setbacks, both Marshall and his legacy appeared not only alive but invincible.

The great civil rights advocate had helped demolish the ramparts of segregation, braved threats to his life to defend poor blacks in remote towns, cleared the way for minority groups to cast their ballots, helped black and white schoolchildren learn to live with one another, and fought hard for the constitutional rights that protect *all* U.S. citizens. "We weren't fighting for Afro-Americans," Marshall said about his remarkable struggle for civil rights that spanned six decades. "We were fighting for the heart of the entire nation."

Other Books You Might Enjoy Reading

1. Aldred, Lisa. *Thurgood Marshall: Supreme Court Justice.* Chelsea House Publishers, 1990. (YA)
2. Feinberg, Barbara Silberdick. *The Constitution Yesterday, Today, and Tomorrow.* Scholastic Press, 1978. (YA)
3. Fenderson, Lewis H. *Thurgood Marshall: Fighter for Justice.* McGraw-Hill and Rutledge Books, 1969. (YA)
4. Goldman, Roger, and David Gallen, eds. *Thurgood Marshall: Justice For All.* Carroll & Graf, 1992.
5. Hughes, Langston, Milton Meltzer, and C. Eric Lincoln. *A Pictorial History of Black Americans.* Crown, (Fifth revised edition) 1983.
6. Quayle, Louise. *Martin Luther King, Jr.: Dreams for a Nation.* Fawcett Columbine (Great Lives Series), 1989. (YA)
7. Stevens, Leonard A. *Equal! The Case of Integration vs. Jim Crow.* Coward, McCann & Geoghegan, 1976. (YA)
8. Woodward, Bob, and Scott Armstrong. *The Brethren: Inside the Supreme Court.* Simon and Schuster, 1979.